AF422853

Permanent Scars

Markus Cuttino

Permanent Scars

Printed in the United States of America

Published by Cuttino's Clubhouse

Produced by Create and Blossom Studios

www.createandblossomstudios.com

ISBN hardcover 979-8-9871605-0-3

ISBN e-book   979-8-9871605-1-0

First Edition, December 2022

CONTENTS

DEDICATION

To my father (Rodriquez Cedric Collins), my grandfather (Joe Edward Cuttino), and to my great-grandparents (Joe Nathan Cuttino & Bernice Cuttino). May you all rest in peace, love.

INTRODUCTION: JOURNAL

S car noun: a mark remaining (as on the skin) after injured tissue has healed. – Merriam-Webster Dictionary

What do permanent scars mean to me? Permanent scars entail those challenging, tough, and even traumatic events that I label life-changing forever. Let's set the record straight and make it known that, unfortunately, permanent scars don't ride the coattail of a specific group of people, race, religion, or gender, but it's for everyone. It's not just a simple scratch on the surface of your skin, a long day at work, or even failing a college exam. It's not even the "oh shit" moments or the "it's not one thing, it's another thing" moments. Those are challenging too, but I'm talking about the events that make you wonder how you would overcome them and move on. I'm talking about the dark head spaces filled with tears while you feel like you are fighting demons and want everything to be over. You want these moments to be erased. The events where you nearly or did lose everything, being stuck with having to figure out how to get back up and fight again, that left you traumatized and permanently scarred and is just too much to bear or revisit mentally. "Why me? Why me?" is all you can continue to ask yourself. If they knew, right?

Permanent scars are called life, and even though this may sound crazy during challenging seasons of your life, it very much so is what you make it. Permanent Scars is my memoir that's told through my lens with various permanent scars that changed my life. It includes the good, the bad, and the ugly. First, we must know that these scars are traumatic events that affect us and are here to stay. Often, they are the cause and effect of our character and who we become due to things we have engaged in or been through. I've learned to channel these events and face my problems head-on through therapy, love, my go-to, reading, and meditation. So, before joining me on my memoir journey, take a second to ask yourself, what brings you happiness and mental peace? What makes your heart truly melt and overflow with joy? Now that you have those answers, Let's begin.

"What will you do with your pain? Will you let it break or redefine you?"

– Eric Thomas.

CHAPTER

1

MAY 18, 1995 GEORGETOWN MEMORIAL HOSPITAL, SOUTH CAROLINA

Dear someone who may read this one day over a glass of your favorite chilled drink with two ice cubes to be exact and your favorite cigar. Well, maybe that's not you, but that's what I'm doing as I write these words in my new favorite notebook. Have you ever thought about the days when life seemed easier than others? When you were overwhelmed with joy versus the time in your life when everything looked as if you're locked in a permanent seat of an emotional roller coaster? It may feel like life is bound to self-destruct at any given day now. I, for one, do miss the times we often referred to as "the good ole days" when I was a kid. I had no responsibilities whatsoever. What's stress? Most importantly, I didn't need a job. Being a child with my favorite piece of candy at my elementary school, my favorite bicycle my parents got me for my birthday—the one with a red bow on the front of it—was everything. I remember receiving invitations to friends' birthday parties, because that's what we did as kids growing up in my day. We loved action figures, playing in the dirt for some odd reason, and the getting latest Game Cube or PlayStation system we begged Santa Clause for. Have you ever gone to the middle of the mall, sat on the neighborhood Santa Clause lap while your parents were taking pictures and your only concern was convincing Santa that you were a good child, and this was your enormous Christmas list and why you should receive everything listed?

Dear someone who may read this one day thinking at this very moment, "Boy, have times changed," what were *your* happy days like as a child? Can you remember them by any chance? These are the moments we sometimes wish we cherished just a little harder and a little while longer. Oh man, I remember the days of coming home and getting off the Browns Ferry Elementary school bus in Georgetown, South Carolina. The sweetest neighborhood bus driver happens to be my little brother's bus driver right now. Isn't that something?

My grandmother knew the way to my heart after school was a nicely smothered peanut butter sandwich over Sunbeam King enriched bread, while I watched one of my two favorite cartoons—

Rocket Power or Tom and Jerry. That's right, those were my must haves with absolutely NO JELLY! Is anyone with me, or am I the only one who hates jelly? How long did it take us to realize that one of our favorite cartoons, Tom & Jerry, consisted of two characters who did not speak at all? Hopefully, this is not new to anyone, as I'm writing and laughing aloud. Take a minute to think about your after-school routine. What were your must-haves that you could just not wait to get home and get your hands on or perhaps get your eyes on? Maybe it was to get out of those school clothes, jump right into your play clothes, and scream "Mom, I'm going over (insert your friends name) house!" while running out the front door. In today's time, 2022, do parents still separate school clothes from play clothes? I remember going outside to play hide-n-go-seek or jumping on my mongoose bicycle to ride around our little country hood. Some people may refer to it as the sticks, Route 4 Oatland, South Carolina. Now anyone from these areas know exactly what it looks like, double-wide trailers, for the most part, a few brick houses, the elder's farmland, and their tractor to include hog and pig pins, a few dogs roaming around, the top hustlers hanging out in the popular yards and one small candy store and the lady who makes your favorite Icey's. That's right, Smoothie King doesn't have anything on the hood candy store with the cup Icey. And yes, we do have to ride to the nearest town for gas, fast food, and Walmart. As far as you can remember, these specific happy-go-lucky moments you encountered growing up as a child may have crossed your mind. You wondered if this is what life is about, then living is quite easy. Suddenly, boom, those permanent scars we don't even realize at the time begin to strike here and there slowly but surely.

I remember it like it was yesterday. I used to hang out at my cousin's house. We'd run around in the yard tossing the football around because, of course, in every neighborhood like the one I come from, you were only trying to do one of two things. You dreamed of being a basketball or football star. Now, back to the story inside of a story. We were outside my cousin's house tossing the football around, and suddenly, a ton of black smoke began to cloud the sky. It looked like a big storm was on its way. The sky rapidly got dark. The smoke was gray and black and had the scent of something burning, and not the sweet-smothered BBQ smell of a freshly lit grill either. I wondered what was going on. We jumped on our bikes and followed the direction the smoke was coming from. It led us to a long dirt road with a burning double-wide trailer.

News spread fast in the hood, or everyone was just nosey, because people were coming out of nowhere. Suddenly, as I was coming to a halt staring down this dirt road, it hit me. The dark smoke was coming from my home, and it was burning it away to shambles. My grandparent's double-wide trailer was on fire. I sat on my bicycle, staring off into the days and watching the flames grow bigger and taller until the trailer was covered. The good thing was everyone was safe. There was no harm to anyone. Up until this day, I have no idea how the fire even started.

I believe the story goes like this. My aunt was in the kitchen cooking at the time, and a fire broke out. After writing this, I'll ask her whether she remembers this day. Maybe it was a permanent scar for her as well. I mean, she was involved in a fire that could have been life-threatening.

Honestly, as a kid, I'm not sure if I even thought about much at that very moment. We were, in fact, homeless. Despite my grandparents losing everything, I think my biggest concern was that all my clothes and favorite toys were gone. You know how in the movies, something tragic happens, and one person screams, "Please, noooo!" That gave me a sense of hopelessness and, without a doubt, unknowingly at the time, my first permanent scar and that me wondering, "Now what?" But as the good book says, life goes on.

To every child- I dream of a world where you can laugh, dance, sing, learn, live in peace and be happy"

– Malala Yousafzai.

CHAPTER

2

T IS FOR TRAUMATIZED

Well, life in fact did go on. I guess that's the funny thing about time. It doesn't stop and start again, because you're going through something and just need things to slow up a bit, while you gather yourself. So, life went on. I guess we weren't technically homeless. In fact, we just went right across the street to my great-grandparent's house (my grandad parents). Some would call it a blessing to still have all my grandparents alive and healthy, which in fact was very much so true. Living with my great grandparents for those three years was different. You know, elders tend to have their routine and that's what they're sticking to. They believe what they believe and the majority of the time what they say goes and there's no changing their opinion on that. We adjusted, and I grew to like it.

There are two things I can distinctly remember about my great grandfather. He absolutely loved humming. I was young of course, so I couldn't actually name the songs he was humming. But, if there was an award-winning category for humming, he would have won it. It was just so natural like humming was supposed to be his thing, man. I wish you could've heard it. I remember the sunny days when I'd sit outside with my grandfather—him wearing his straw-- hat while he'd hum away. He'd take out his pocketknife to peel and sharpen small tree branches. If you know, you know. And if not, maybe this was a deep country thing straight out of Route 4, South Carolina.

I can see my great-grandparents now in the old days during farming season. My great-grandfather jumps up on his tractor and turns the key. It took a couple of times, until it fires right up with a small burst of smoke from the muffler pipes. As my great-grandfather is plying the field to lay his corn, my great-grandmother is calling "Markus" in her sweet little voice to come and help her pick her cabbage and peas. Have you ever had to shell peas and peel them after they've been picked? Boy it is time consuming, but as a seven-, eight-, and nine-year-old at the time, it was fun. Having a farm was just as big of a deal back then as it is today. I mean come to think of it, if there was ever a food shortage in the world it wouldn't phase us at all. My great-grandmother kept her vegetable jars full. She grew pears, apples, blackberries and had a pecan tree out in the yard. My cousins and I would literally do one of two things; climb the trees and for some odd reason, act like we were up in the clouds overlooking everything. We would also just shake the trees until we had enough of the fruit we wanted to fell. We'd randomly eat from them throughout the day. Have you ever picked some blackberries and filled them in a Ziploc bag with some sugar on top? Now that's what you call good eating. I highly recommended the sugar. We probably were obtaining too much at such an early age. I'm sure it was so unhealthy, but back then, I can hear my great-grandmother telling me now, "What doesn't kill you will only make you stronger." Yup, you cannot change their opinions about a thing and so the unhealthy but oh so good treatment continued, and boy was I am happy camper living with them.

My great-grandfather loved Pepsi and coffee, like seriously it was dear to his heart. The original canned Pepsi filled the refrigerator and that's all he would drink; that or coffee anytime, anywhere and at any given hour of the day, night or day. Personally, I don't think drinking water was a thing back in the early 2000's. I mean who wants to drink water when you can have a nice cold Pepsi with a napkin folded and wrapped around the cane clinching your thirst? I mean that's what my great-grandfather did. He folded a napkin around the can he was drinking out of; I'm assuming because the can was so cold. Wait a second, was my great-grandfather low key on to something and trying to invent the bottle/can holders? He would leave me half a can or half cups of coffee to start. Eventually, I turned into a fiend as a child for some cold Pepsi and warm coffee. The temperature had to be right for me to drink the coffee. Nothing too hot that would burn my tongue, but warm enough where I could drink at my leisure.

Every night when my great-grandfather would go to take a shower, instead of walking down the hall he would slide down the hall. Okay, this maybe a little difficult to explain. Just imagine someone who doesn't necessarily pick their feet up when they're walking so, they're sliding in a sense and making a very distinct sound with. It was the flooring. Back then we had some type of vinyl flooring that's not even close to the fancy wood floors out today. The funny thing is he would only do this in his house slippers. I remember the first time I saw him in motion doing this movement. As he headed for the bathroom, he moved smoothly and in slow motion. I thought the noise was a bit much, but I would stare in disbelief thinking how on God's green earth is he doing that? This seemed cool, and of course, as kids we think everything is cool and just must try it. So, there I went. When no one was looking, I tried to slide-walk in slow motion down the hall. Let's just end it there by saying I could not figure out how he would walk like that for the life of me. Eventually, I gave up trying.

He took excessively long showers. It's also like it was his peace of mind; what he needed. My great-grandmother would come down the hall arriving at the bathroom door calling him "Moddy, Moddy are you okay in there?" And guess what? We cannot forget the hum because if she heard that she knew he was doing just fine.

My grandparents and great-grandmother only disliked the fact that on Monday nights, my excuse for staying up late on a school night was to watch WWE RAW wrestling with my great-grandfather. I mean the show back then literally aired live at 8PM eastern and lasted for three hours. I remember the episode when the Undertaker was coming back from the dead. I was not missing this episode for nothing. I was watching the Undertaker on television as he entered the arena in his smoked out black Harley Davidson wearing his long leather black trench coat with his black cowboy hat. The look on his face that streamed dead man walking with the Undertaker anthem theme song playing in the background. I was a huge fan.

Fast forward to today. I'm not sure If I could tell you if the show still airs. Man, oh Man those were the days. A little bit of Undertaker, Kane, John Cena, Goldberg, Shawn Michael, Triple X, and Rick

Flair. Rey Mysterio was my favorite one jumping off the top ropes. You absolutely could not tell me that this was not the real action taken place in that ring.

While all this was happening, my grandparents were still fighting to find a place they could call home. While staring down an empty dirt road with open field space, "operation grand-parents new home" eventually began. I would watch my grandad get off work from being a manager at Sears in the mechanical maintenance department, head over to this empty field where their double-wide trailer once was and turn into a construction worker. It's no secret that it's very common for people from the country to be extremely good with their hands. They could build and fix just about anything. I still remember them preparing the land for the foundation and pouring brick and concrete into my grandparents' new home. I watched it develop from the blueprint to a beautiful home. This process consisted of walls, windows, flooring, carpet, countertops, cabinets, plumbing, electrical outlets, sheetrock, a roof, and let's not forget, the yellow insulation packed in the walls. I once got stuck in there and had to run and take a shower because it makes you so itchy. This process took three years to build and be moved-in ready. However, they did one important thing: trust the process. Once we moved into my grandparents' new home, I would still walk the dirt road daily after school or ride my bike across the street to my great-grandparents.

However, things were starting to change drastically. Things were slowing down at their end, specifically with my great-grandfather.

The huge farm surrounded by wire to keep the deer and other roaming animals out was eventually beginning to turn into just grass. The sunny days of the tractor putting a couple of times to fire up with a small could of smoke from the muffler pipes weren't happening anymore. What was going on? What was wrong, grandpa? Why aren't you humming as you used to or sitting outside in your favorite chair, straw hat, and pocketknife? Now, I had no idea at the time. He was getting older and was becoming a sick man of a few words. Now he had less and less to say. His face was a little narrower.

He would chill in his recliner. I didn't know what would happen next would change my life forever.

April 21st, 2007, at 81 years old, my great-grandfather took his last breath. It included funeral preparations on what seemed to be a regular day in the life of a sixth grader at Carvers Bay middle school. Back then, I didn't have a cellphone, and I wasn't picked up from school, getting off the school bus to find out the news. I just remembered the look on my grandfather's face. The face a grown man makes when he's just lost his father, the expression a grown man makes when his mother is now a widow but come to think of it, my grandad siblings pretty much all looked up to him, and I never actually remember him shedding a tear in front of me. He was strong for his mother, loved ones, sisters, and brothers. How did I feel? Again, I'm not quite sure how I felt or if I thought everyone was supposed to live forever. At the time, I'm not quite sure, but I do know that I was attending my first funeral, my great-grandfather was gone, and the family was devastated, and that day I cried like a baby. This can't be real. How did my great-grandmother find it in her to drive on staying alone? The world may never know. Black women sometimes must be so strong and feel so lonely. She must've had many nights of crying herself to sleep.

There are so many things that I miss about my great-grandfather. Even today, I would much rather have one more round of hide-n-go-seek through the sugarcane and corn on the cob trees on the farm where the bushings grew so tall you're lost inside until you find your way out on the other end. Yup, one more foot race with my friends and cousins to the other end. If only this would bring you back. If only I could taste that coffee. I got the chance to drink coffee with my great-grandfather one more time. Little did I know at that time this hurtful broken feeling that began to overwhelm me as time went on was yet another permanent scar.

"There are wounds that never show on the body that are deeper and more hurtful than anything that bleeds"-

Laurell K. Hamilton

CHAPTER

3

THE GOOD THE BAD AND THE UGLY

A pril 10th, 2008, marked eleven days from exactly a year of my great-grandfather's passing. There's something about the month of April. And honestly, this is the toughest part of the book to write.

Fourteen years ago on one Thursday, as I'm getting up preparing for a normal day at middle school, I had no idea that this day would be the epitome of the worse day of my life. It's like the horror movie you wish you never watched and the reality you wish was all a dream. No human could ever prepare for or see something like this coming.

There I was in gym class near ending. It was the last period of the day for me. Of course, I had on something fly; it was the Rocawear clothing brand co-founded by Damon Dash and Jay-Z. There was a Citi trends department store in the nearest town that sold all the fly clothes back then and you could catch everyone in the latest gear shopping there.

We must've been shooting around in the gym for class that day. It was nothing major going on, but all of a sudden, the gym teacher came up to me and said they needed to see you up at the front office. Instantly everyone goes, "Oooooooo!!" There I was looking confused and wondering what I did. Is it just me or do people naturally have a mini panic attack when someone says they have something important to tell or show you? I always wonder why they couldn't have said it right then and there, stead of putting my brain in a frenzy.

I pushed the office door open and there was my grandmother along with my principal and staff. I'm looking at everyone and everyone is looking at me with what looked like an expression of empathy and sympathy. At 12 years old, we don't know how to read body language. My principal then says so humbly, "Markus let's head on back to my office." So, we walk on to the back and take a seat, as he softly closes the door behind us. I'll never forget the words he started the conversation with -- "You know, sometimes in life things happen that we often don't understand."

As he's talking and trying to gather his words, he went from looking me directly in my eyes to kind of talking with his head down. As he's looking back up at me a tear begins to fall from his eyes as he says, "Your father was involved in a motorcycle accident today on his way home from work, Fort Stewart, Georgia (Army Base)" As a little boy things were not resonating with me quickly enough because quite frankly, I was still kind of lost. "Is he alright being he in the hospital any bruises, anything? Just like that, within a split second, my grandmother could not take it anymore. She burst into tears saying my dad didn't make it and that he was gone. She must've said he did not make it five more times before it started to hit me and sink in. I held my head down, shaking my head as the tears began to overflow. I couldn't help it even if I wanted to.

Usually, I would tell someone who may read this one day, that I didn't know how I felt, or I didn't know how to feel. Let's start by saying this feeling is one I would not wish on my worst enemy. I was crushed. My heart broke into pieces. I was sick, throwing up, mute, stuck, and dreaming. I thought, wake me up when it's over. I questioned the creator from up above. Those are some of the words that come to mind, as I sat back and tried to replay that feeling over and over again. Some days, I still question why? Honestly, I absolutely hate thinking about it and if there was any possible way, I could tell my story without mentioning it, I absolutely without a doubt would. Yes, I still randomly break down and cry some nights. Sometimes I wonder if he was here what would be different. I wish I could lean on him for when I'm in doubt. We're only human and losing a parent is by far to me the toughest battle life has to offer.

Imagine a drunk person who's torn up from the floor up. That was me. I just could not seem to get my legs up from under me. My knees were weak. Walking to the car holding on to my grandmother seemed forever. On the ride home I remember just thinking this can't be true, this isn't happening. I wanted to give my dad a call and tell him about this crazy rumor that was out back home about him in South Carolina that he died from a fatal motorcycle accident. Well, I guess not even I could hold on to this for so long because his phone never rings. My dad never answered, while the story rapidly grew over the Georgia news and can still be Googled. Talk about the power of Google, huh.

The headline was *Staff Sergeant Rodriquez Cedric Collins fatal motorcycle accident.* No one had a bigger Kool-aid smile like he had with a unique great big laugh to match. No more exciting conversations about what we were going to do all summer.

At my grandparents' house, I recall my grandfather saying he had a dream about my dad the night before. Now if that was not a coincidence, I don't know what is. I rushed to my room, sat down in my small blue chair and it hit me all over again. I could just not stop crying. You ever cried so much that your head begins to hurt, that was me a pounding head, a snotty nose and a wet face from so many tears for the rest of the night. But wait, my nana (my dad's mother) I haven't got the chance to speak to her yet.

Now before going any further, let me tell you about my nana. This lady is a legend across Andrews, South Carolina and you would think she's *everyone's* grandmother because everyone across town just simply calls her Nana. She feeds everyone and *everyone* wants a plate of that good soul food. Where we come from, cooking soul food is mainly a daily thing. We never ate fast food every day. Maybe because we simply did not really have fast-food restaurants to choose from besides the famous McDonalds.

Nana would literally cross you up on the basketball court up until she was in her early 60's and pull up for the three pointers. She could shoot your eyes out and still, even though she may not run around as much on the court with the guys. Today, she still loves basketball. Go Lebron James, right?

In a legendary hood called "C-City," all the guys would host big basketball games at my nana house to play b-ball with her. Her genes are mag-ni-fi-cent. Everyone respected her and loved it. People wondered, "How was she this old moving like that?" I'm telling you, it was a sight to see.

The court was full of dirt with a wooden backboard, a metal pole that was planted in the ground, a rim and a ripped-up net. Coming from where we come from, we just made things work. All the kids were raised by Nana and were always over at Nana's house, so the same applies to you, no matter the age. If you ever get the precious chance to meet her one day, just call her Nana.

My dad's side of the family is from a small town in South Carolina called Andrews, nicknamed *The Little A*. In about ten-fifteen minutes, you could be in the town and out on the other side. There's nothing big about it at all. It's a tiny place many people call home that has a nice legendary chicken spot known as Super Chick that has probably been around longer than most of the people who will read this book. They are known for their potato wedges and chicken.

Come to think of it, I guess I will proclaim right here right now that I'm my Nana's favorite grandchild. Why? Because all my cousins who I love dearly probably won't read this line. I said all of that to describe how this precious humble lady must've felt inside. I remember arriving at my aunt's house in Andrews watching Nana crying and screaming, "He's gone, he's gone. He's gone. My baby is gone!" She repeatedly cried squeezing me so tight for so long. I could instantly tell that I was all I had left for my family to remind them of my dad.

People would always remind me that they knew him and that I looked just like him. He was the super glue that held the family together. He encouraged everyone, gave friends and family things to look forward to, was motivational. With him being gone, you could see the devastation from the family. His loss created a void. We lost hope, as if the creator had knocked life out of anything we all had left. Let's just describe the month of April in 2008 as pure trash. I mean it was horrible; a complete living hell on earth.

Why can't I sleep? Why don't I have an appetite? Why is everyone trying to tell me they know how I feel through words of comfort? Just because your dad died when you were twelve also and your mom had to carry you out his funeral doesn't mean you could possibly know how I felt. I mean, thank you but no thank you.

After the family funeral we had to head to Fort Stewart for the Armies funeral and that's where I got introduced to what's called *roll call*. The First Sergeant called everyone to attention in the platoon and began to sound off their names. They respond, "Here, First Sergeant!" and then oh boy and then oh boy when they get to the name of the person who passed they call his name with so much power so much authority that shakes the room something like this Staff Sergeant Collins! Waits a few, Staff Segreant Collins! As the tears and snickering began to fill the room from the family and other soldiers, he gives it one more try. "Staff Sergeant Collins!" With no response the rifle gun shots begin to cock and unload sounding off in unison outside the building. I'm twenty-seven years old today. Reliving these moments when I was a young child still send chills through my body. They say time heals pain. I'll be the first to tell you that's not true. If so, tell me why these tears keep falling. Yes, I was an emotional wreck, but I remember the birthday parties, the school clothes shopping, him buying me my first flip phone the razor in the 7th grade and me thinking I was a bad mutha *watch your mouth!* Every summer I would head to stay with my dad and that's where I first found my love for Texas. He was stationed at Fort Hood, Texas, before bringing him to Fort Stewart, GA.

The central Texas area is not too far from the major cities in Texas. It's within three hours or so driving distance at the most. Later in this book, you'll also find out that Fort Hood, Texas was also my first duty station in the Army. Is that a coincidence or what? I remember it like it was yesterday. I spent my fourth-grade year summer out in Texas before moving on to the fifth grade the following school year. There was just something different about Texas. It could have been the heat that played tricks on me to where

I found myself in a pool almost every day that summer. I thought my dad was the coolest Army soldier in the world-- top tier G.I Joe.

Now, if you're not familiar with the famous military haircut, especially in the early 2000's, this was it. A low-cut fade with bald sides and back was in and with a clean face, no facial hair you could spot a man that was in the military from a mile away. They would probably be wearing a black watch that's in military time and walked like a robot. As a child I wanted to be just like my father down to the haircut, the walk, and the whole swag. Surprisingly, guess who's lucky day it was, because my dad was a barber too. I'm guessing it was just a side hustle cutting all the soldier's hair in his unit and around the base.

My first G.I. Joe haircut was everything to me. Every few days I would bother my dad to freshen it up and fortunately for me no matter how tired he was after work, I would sit in his barber chair, and he would. I mean, yes, even though I was in elementary school and haven't absolutely the slightest idea about life yet, I do have an image to uphold, right? Well that very summer knowing absolutely nothing about life went out the window and morals began.

Saturday was just a normal day around the house after chores, which consisted mainly of taking out the trash and keeping the room clean. After chores, we received a weekly allowance and I usually ended up at Dollar General with a crispy twenty-dollar bill in my hand. We sat in the car and my dad handed me twenty dollars and said "When we go in there, buy anything you want."

I replied with excitement, "Anything?"

He simply replied "Yes."

As a kid with twenty dollars, I initially thought I could buy the whole store with that twenty-dollar bill. I mostly wanted lots and lots of candy and nothing else. Long story short, that's exactly what I did; buy lots of candy and one deck of playing cards for a game of *I Declare War*. "If you've never played this game, this is how it goes.

You simply split the deck evenly with your opponent and each of you draw cards saying I-De-clare-War. Once you land on *war* that card is flipped and whoever has the bigger card wins that round and collects all the cards. You repeat this, until someone is out of card; that's the loser. We got to the register with my ton of candy and one deck of playing cards and I think the total was somewhere around nineteen dollars and eighty four cents leaving me with sixteen cents to spare. My dad said nothing as we paid and walked out of the store, we finally, made it back home, which seemed to take forever. I was ready to dive into my candy, but little did I know there was a lesson waiting for me at the dinner table. As we both took a seat, he began.

"Son, how much money do you have left over from your allowance I gave you?"

I honestly did not even know what I did with the sixteen cents, but I knew I had candy to fuel that sugar fetish that was running inside the majority of every little kid in the world. He explained, "You worked for twenty dollars by doing your chores and within ten minutes of being paid, you were broke again with nothing."

Now of course as a ten-year-old kid I thought this was a little harsh and my dad was a pain in the you know what.

"I mean, I'm a kid dad. What exactly did you want me to do with the money," I said.

His response was the most shocking thing to me.

He said, "Save it. I told you to buy anything you want out the store that the twenty dollars could cover, but I never told you to spend it *all* or that you had to. Now what are you going to do until next Friday? Until your next allowance rolls around?"

Well, the simple answer for me was to just simply ask him. "I'll just ask you to buy it for me. If I want a McDonald's happy meal, I'll just ask you to buy it for me," I replied.

Long story short, I didn't get that McDonald's happy meal, until the following weekend when I got my allowance for doing my chores. At the time, I didn't quite understand, but he was teaching me the value of money, without intentionally coming out and saying that's what he was doing. He was showing me the importance of always saving twice as much as you spend. He understood so many gems to life. He taught me early on how to pray. I can hear him now telling me to always, always, always pray for wisdom and discipline. As a child I had no idea about the lessons he was teaching and the moral's he was instilling in me, until later in life when I began to use them to my benefit. I thank my father, to this day. I will always make sure in my prayers I'm asking for wisdom and discipline.

Later, my pops came down on orders for a permanent change of station, which brought him to Fort Stewart, Georgia. By this time, I was in the sixth grade and was turning into a little man-- at least I thought so anyway. That summer before starting the seventh grade, my Saturday routine consisted of early mornings being waken up around seven or eight in the morning, as I'm stumbling into walls with my eyes half close trying to make it to the bathroom to wash my face and brush my teeth. I had to go running with him in the neighborhood, and that was not an option. We would stretch and then he would say, "You ready?" I could not stop running. It was absolutely forbidden even though the neighborhood had a huge hill on the street. We would run all the way up and then once we made it to the top, I'd be completely exhausted with my legs feeling like noodles. They could completely give out at any moment. He would say, "You tired?"

"Ugh, yes dad.",

I suffered with severe asthma as a child and was in and out the hospital. I had to use a nebulizer at night daily before bed and an inhaler throughout my day. I wanted to remind him of that but he already knew it. Running in place or in a small circle, until I was ready to keep going was hard. I hated it so much, before I began to like it. I was not about to let my dad down. This man meant everything to me. My legs would literally have to detach itself from my body before I stopped running so when I was tired, I would just stop and jog in place while catching my breath.

At the time, he was dropping gems without realizing it. In life, we get tired, and we want to give up. Sometimes we are put in uncomfortable situations, but it's easy to quit the hard thing. All you have to do is keep going when you can and just say *to hell with this*. You have to activate beast mode which would give you the ability to keep going through the obstacles in life. That's the tough part, and that's exactly what he wanted me to do. No matter what, keep going.

"I will. I can. I must".

On Saturday's after all of that, I must come home and help him cut the grass in the yard with the push lawnmower and weed the edges. Honestly, I grew to like it and just thought it was mainly about spending time with my pops, as we capped the day off with one of our two favorite movies, *Biker Boys* and the first *Fast and the Furious*. We had dreams of building a muscle old school race car Dodge Charger like Dominic Toretto (Vin Diesel in the film) and his dad did in the movie once I was older. Unfortunately, due to his untimely demise in my upcoming school year, we never got to build our race car.

I do hold on to the many things we talked about like how my parents met, where and when I was born. My dad never hid nothing from me. I have stories for days about the mistakes he made growing up and the steps he took to change his life. We would talk about the different stories for hours, whether it was at the drive-in movie theater we would go to or a late night out in the garage just talking and laughing. This man was truly the greatest of all time and I know the lessons he was trying to teach me all along at a young age was all for a great reason. Later that school year when the traumatizing event of his death occurred, I found out why. I won't act like dealing with this has been easy, but his wisdom has helped a ton and as you know it, another permanent scar grew, but still life goes on.

Who's the kid now running all over Andrews, South Carolina straight out of Baltimore, Maryland that has my auntie head over heels in puppy love? I don't know what Nana and my grandparents would call young teens who thought they were so in love. They'd call it puppy love. Yes, that love affair between those two started back in middle and high school and they're still together to this day. So, I guess you could say there is a such thing as love at first sight or high school sweethearts. Now, I never said that they probably didn't go through hell and back with each other. All I said was that they're still together 30 plus years later so *love* has got to be a real thing and should count for something. I guess my auntie is what you would call the definition of a *rider* or maybe it was his demeanor and swag that kept her around, you know the north is so much different from the south. It's just like night and day down to the vocabulary and accent followed by their three kids my cousins, so who knows maybe that's another story for my aunt to tell.

Some knew my uncle as Benjamin, Ben Dawg, and B.G. He later became known as DJ Buzzurk. There's one thing for certain; he was a pure hustler and I loved every bit out of it. Early on, my aunt and uncle developed this whole family bonding fun day thing where on Fridays we would all go somewhere fun for the kids. One of those trips landed us at the skating ring where I chipped my front tooth. Let's just say my cousin had no idea how to skate and as he's falling to the ground on the skating rink floor, guess who just so happen to be near as he tried to catch his balance by tugging on my shoulder? I assumed it just a natural reaction, but boy did I get the short end of the stick. I fell flat on my face and busted my grill. I had a chipped tooth. The pain hit instantly, as I held my mouth. We still had fun even though I had a chipped tooth that got fixed the upcoming week.

My uncle Ben was one smooth fella, not soft spoken but just a little and he meant business and was about his money for sure. Remember the lesson early on about my dad teaching me the value of money with the twenty-dollar bill? Well, I knew one thing for sure. My uncle had a boat load of it and my eyes were locked in on how he was making all this money with all these different cars, a crew of men and women, a club and more. I mean, it was like it was a never-ending thing. He pressed a button and thousands just magically appeared in his hand or something. I distinctively remember my cousins would use the house phone if he wasn't home to call his cellphone and ask for something and it would show up at the house instantly. Wow, my dad never had those magical powers. My cousin asked for a four-wheeler from his dad on Christmas Eve and guess what appeared at the house on Christmas day? You guessed it; a four-wheeler on top of dirt bikes, scooters, and mopeds. There was literally enough for everyone in the area to come over, have fun and ride. I had never seen nothing like it, but I still had no idea where all this money was coming from.

I knew what the word around town was, but was it true? Was my uncle really the biggest drug dealer around moving weight at the time? Are the stories true? He received shipments from this place and that place, this state and that state, this boating dock, and that boating dock. My uncle was an American Gangster, and I loved every second of it.

Now, where did I get that name? Years ago BET would televise a show called American Gangster which displayed the glamorous lifestyle of big-time drug dealers, the fabulous life they lived as they provided for those around them, and the finest of everything. Now, what I missed was the most important part which was the lessons taught by each American Gangster who would see the light of day again after a lengthy prison sentence. They told their story about their empire and how it came to an end-- the fall of it all. Besides this won't happen to my uncle anyway I mean you've got to be a mastermind to run this type of operation at this level.

I would always wonder why he always wore new clothing. This guy never skipped a beat. The interesting thing about it all is I never actually saw with my own two eyes him commit any crimes or do anything illegal. I was always very defensive when it came down to my uncle and had no idea what the police and haters would be talking about. Police never actually caught him doing anything illegal either. When you combine conspiracy with the Federal Drug Enforcement

Administration (DEA) and people who want what you have, there's almost a hundred percent chance that you're fighting an uphill losing battle. Save yourself the headache and just go work legally in life for anything you may inspire to have. Now, of course, I was not crazy. Coming from where we come from it was not hard to tell who was doing what around the town, or who ran the best crews, kept a pocket full of money, or who's name you'd know from state to state. This meant you were somebody who was well respected; you were at the top and everyone wanted what you had. Now, here is what I did not understand. In the mist of all of this, after the fun times with family and friends and everything you do for them people *still* may not like you.

I vividly remember the summer of 2008. It was the year I was heading to the eighth grade. My cousin and I got the chance to ride with his dad and my uncle in his sprinter van to one of the biggest car shows of the year. It was out in the country. Now if you aren't familiar with what a car show is, it's when the best of the best come out. It features the best of old school cars, the cleanest vehicles, battles of the loudest sound music, Harley Davidsons, motorcycles, bike and car clubs—you name it. These types of fun events are dressed to impress with food trucks lined up waiting to take your order. My cousin and I felt like the man of the year that day riding with his dad and crew. They were known as C-City Boyz. This represented the turf they were from.

On the ride there, I remember smoke filling the air and wondering about the smell. It was cloudy in there. Today, my friend, that would be known as the aroma of *good gas*, or at least that's what people who smoke call it. Not to mention, he was a huge Gucci Mane fan. I'm still unsure how my uncle's cars got to the car show, but everyone knew they were his. Maybe he was interested in drawing little attention to himself, but that would never work.

The females loved him, and my auntie hated it. She would always remind everyone of her position and that she was the boss lady. I mean, you had to see it. If you ever wondered what a real-life Bonnie and Clyde looked like firsthand, this was it at its finest.

My favorite car was always the old school box chevy painted candy of the gamecock's colorway and the logo on the hood of the car sitting on 28's with tv screens so big you could mount them as a living room tv in your house. However, shortly after that great night, we would need more preparation for what would happen next. In about three to six months later, the rise and fall of my uncle's enterprise would begin to take a turn for the worse. Did you really think your competition would let you make all this money for this long?

I was in social studies class one day. I got off the school bus, entered my grandparents' house, and she was reading the newspaper. I gave the greeting of the day, and she softly said, "Your uncle was arrested this morning."

I replied with a shocked facial expression," Huh, what happened?"

Then, she began to show me the newspaper article headlining this huge drug bust that took place in Andrews, SC. The types of drugs, the amount, who was in the house, and the amount of cash they took off each person were unbelievable. Now, in the midst of all of this, I'm not sure if I was sad that my uncle had been arrested or excited because he made the county newspaper article. The amount of cash they took off his person was very impressive. I did not even know walking around with that kind of money was possible. Maybe I was thinking something like, "You go, Unc!" Now, I know what you may think, but could you blame me? My dad had already engraved the value of money in my head, and on the other hand, my uncle had what seemed to be boatloads of it that would never end. I'm sorry, guys, but my love for money by this time was at an all-time high. It never crossed my mind that he could be in serious trouble and facing some serious time.

This arrest spread the city like wildfire, B.G being sick at one of his crew members' houses, staying overnight, not making it home, and this one bad hiccup would cost him something money could not buy. He and the crew members who were there would all make bail, paying a pricey bond. Before we knew it, the DEA would knock at my aunt's door again to make it known they were looking for Benjamin Richardson. At the time, he was not home. He was never in one place for very long, which made his state arrest shocking to everyone. He was never the type of guy who would stand still long. At this point, he knew it was nothing he could do once the DEA was on his back. He just decided to turn himself in. I never questioned what that ride was like between my aunt and uncle because no one thought he was about to do a lengthy sentence. I mean, it's an indictment, and they caught him with nothing right, but believe me, along with conspiracy and other things, they have their ways of sticking things.

My uncle was different, maybe a little flashy, but still humble. He never made excuses for his wrongdoings. He never pointed the finger or blamed anyone else for his actions. That could affect his sentence being overturned when President Barack Obama passed a few laws in his favor. In his case, a life sentence to serving about ten years in federal prison would be considered a blessing, right? During those ten years, if he ever got down, the family didn't say it. That was his way of accepting responsibility. Nights may have been tough because he lost his brother and more family members while inside.

The first couple of years of his sentence was, let's say, hell for me. Maybe I'm exaggerating just a little, but it was tough. This was another permanent scar in February 2009. It was approximately a year of my father's passing in April of 2008 and about two years after my great-grandfather's passing in April 2007.

Permanent scars were becoming a yearly trend, and I had no idea why this was happening to me. Some people are just flat right out now as haters, and they would always tease, saying, your uncle is never getting out of prison, so I could only imagine what my cousins were going through as this also came with a change of lifestyle. Someone I looked up to had gone again, and I was unsure if he was ever coming home, honestly. We would email each other through a platform called Corrlink. He would always need the spread of the NFL games on Sundays. I did not know what it meant then, but today I can imagine he needed to see his favorite team for possible games he was trying to bet on inside.

During those ten years, we talked less and less due to circumstances, but my love for him never changed. Ten years later, he would return home to his family, and I imagined his first thought would be about how life is different.

In our first conversation, I'm sure he was excited to be back around his kids and loved ones, but he was still normal and soft-spoken. He did not express himself like a guy who had just done ten years behind bars. I thought he was supposed to be jumping up and down or doing jumping jacks, but he was quite the opposite. Maybe a little institutionalized. When we talked, I wanted to know how he felt about things. I wondered, after all that time, if he would change anything. Surprisingly, he said he wouldn't change a thing; that prison was known as a bad thing but may not always be the case if you somehow used it to your advantage. I've never been, so I could not say that he was right or wrong, but I couldn't see how going to prison was not such a bad thing either. He said the prison had saved him, and he saw things differently now.

He would not change his life, not at all. He lived his life to the fullest, a line he would always quote before his fall. He told me he remembered days of him buying kilos and making twenty-seven thousand a day in profit sometimes, that he never honestly knew how much money he had because it was just fast money daily. He would spend money just as fast as he made it taking care of everyone, so he never had any idea how much money he had. I wonder what ever happened to the pimp cup he had in his club engraved "The World Is Yours" maybe that was for the females he would also have in his crew, who dressed nice and took advantage of men. To someone who may read this one day, I will leave you with this about him; he always lived up to everything he said he would do and was very wise, even though the route he previously chose may have made you think otherwise. He was adamant once he came home about the trucking industry as it was what he studied inside and wanted to do if he ever got a chance at freedom again.

Going on about five years free, receiving his commercial driver's license with a few years of experience, he is one of the best truck drivers I know today, and boy, I know plenty. He seems to love working, which is quite funny since he never had to work, but now he loves family, spending quality time with his grandkids, providing, and making memories. Still, he and my auntie are rocking it like Bonnie and Clyde. Now is a good time to take a minute and identify one of my favorite words to date, perseverance, defined by Merriam-Webster dictionary as "continued effort to do or achieve something despite difficulties, failure, or opposition." Was I displaying perseverance in my character unknowingly at such an early age? Then, later in life, it became one of my favorite words once I found out what It meant. Who remembers the last famous fight, titled "Thrilla in Manilla," between Muhammad Ali, aka The Louisville Lip, and Joe Frazier, aka Smokin Joe, back in 1975? I didn't because I, for one, was not even born yet. However, from what I read and watched on YouTube, this fight was sensational and changed the trajectory of boxing forever.

In the third fight of these rivals who tried to tear each other apart in the ring, who would win the tiebreaker and be titled the world champion? Muhammad Ali would remain champion, but that was not what kept me from reading and learning about this famous fight, "Thrilla in Manilla." I knew that closing out the tenth round Joe Frazier had just about tried everything giving Ali just about all he had left in the tank, blow for blow, hoping that the next punch would land and send Ali diving facing first into the campus. However, what Smoking Joe hoped to happen rather, something much different took place. In the blows coming left and right from Frazier, the

Louisville lip reached to clinch a hug and slow Smokin' Joe down. While doing so, he whispered in his ear, "Is that all you got?" The look on Joe Frazier's face was astonishing, but in disbelief, I'm giving this man all I got. Is he crazy? It was said to be quoted by Muhammad Ali, that knew right then and there by the look in Joe Frazier's eyes when he whispered those words into his ears he had him beat. Who would have thought that a boxing match could be so electrifying to one in comparison to life? Frazier was undoubtedly a permanent scar in this match, and Muhammad Ali was every person who refused to give up on life, who would always get back up and fight back despite difficulties. Could I have given up a long time ago in my early preteen years, or maybe November 3rd, 2009? To someone who may read this one day, you probably think after that line, not again. However, you guessed it right the following year yet again, life had me turned upside down dangling by just one leg and completely just sucking anything I had left inside of me away.

November 3rd, 2009 is the early morning my mother's dad, my grandfather would take his last breath on earth. Although this was the first time I was not at school, I saw it firsthand in my grandparents' house, where colon cancer had taken my grandfather. Let me tell you I don't wish the scream or cries of a widow (my grandmother), a black hearse, and its driver rolling your grandfather out of his home on no one, especially not kids. Everyone was home because this was said to be expected. After my mother made it in from Afghanistan (who still had to return to war after the death of her dad's funeral), I thought that maybe that was all he wanted to see; all of his kids. That following morning, he closed his eyes, never to open them again. While laying there so peacefully, he would leave my grandmother with, "I wouldn't wish this pain on my worst enemy."

My grandfather had been struggling with colon cancer for five years. He had weekly trips to Chemotherapy (a drug treatment that uses powerful chemicals to kill fast-growing cells in your body) and random trips here and there throughout the night of being rushed to the hospital by my grandmother. He fought an outstanding fight but, in the end, could not bear the pain any longer. Being known as the miracle man who doctors originally told he had two weeks to live, then two months, and survived nearly another five years. Could you imagine what it must've been like being my grandfather and the thoughts that were probably going through his head when being told by doctors his life expectancy was two weeks? Devastating, heartbroken, and torn would be an understatement.

We never knew or found out where cancer would strike my grandfather. It's as if it just appeared. But, even through his uphill battle, it never slowed him down. He enjoyed riding around the country in his smooth tan colorway Cadillac or even some days getting on his bicycle, which we would call his caddy, and just riding around the hood. Maybe to him, life slowed down, and he wasn't expected to live anyway, so he was soaking up family time, enjoying the outdoors, a breath of fresh air, and he also cooked more man, oh man, could my grandfather cook them lima beans with neckbones, white rice. Some fried chicken or fried porkchop on the side (back when I ate pork), and we cannot forget the Texas Pete hot sauce.

We loved watching old-time western shows together and loved The Lone Ranger as our favorite. This western icon aired on ABC, Gunsmoke, and the famous Billy The Kid, "quick as a flash" with a gun and known for his witty thievery and outlaw ways, who was eventually gunned down at the age of twenty-one. Before he had to receive chemo treatment, my grandfather owned a pretty nice boat, and on Saturdays, I would find myself being woken up early mornings with him to attend his fishing trip with him and his friends. We would stop for snacks while out on the water and bait from the fish store arriving at the dock, backing the boat down into the water off the trailer, and away we would go out into the ocean. Now, believe it or not, I was young but an A+ fisherman. Why? Because I learned from my grandfather the best.

On one trip while in the water, it seemed that the fish were biting little that day. Then, all of a sudden, I got a tug on my line, then another, and by this time, the tug was so hard that the line was bent almost in the shape of a half U. This particular fish was trying to take the fishing reel right out of the boat with him. So, of course, I had him hooked, and he was trying to get off or away. Now, unless you've ever had a one-on-one battle with a fish, it can get pretty intense, especially if it's the size of a big one. My grandfather would sit back, laugh, and tell me to get him. There's no way I'm letting my grandad down. I'd say, "You're coming home with me tonight, and it's going to be some good eating, baby."

My grandfather made me fight, tug, and reel this fish just about when the fish was almost to the boat and he could see that my noodle arms were getting weak and tired. He'd finally proceed to step in raising the fish to the boat, holding it up by the mouth with his hand. Graaaayyyyyy daddy son that's a big one his grandson had outfished his friends that day, and he was proud. Of course, we talked smack to his friends for the rest of the day, and they were stumped. The fish had to either be a whiting or a spotty fish. We loved filling the coolers with those two types. Then, later we returned home to the yard, cleaned up the boat, scaled and chopped the head off the fish, split the fish, cleaned out its guts, and packed out the freezer with what we would not be cooking that night. Yup, that's right, some good old fish cleaning 101.

On November 3rd, 2009, my grandfather's death stole all of this away from me. How much can one take, let alone experience, back-to-back? So what did little old me do to constantly get my heart shattered into pieces? It happened again when I almost got the pieces picked up and assorted. I questioned our heavenly father God so many times. And truth be told, if I can be honest here, I had lost my faith. I cursed God quietly, but with the Creator seeing all things, I knew he heard me clearly. "How dare you keep taking everyone away from me, my great-grandfather, my father, and now my grandfather." I wanted all the smoke. I was sick and tired of this.

Why did He continue to allow this to happen to me? I would cry out. "Can you hear me up there? Why do you continue to allow this to happen to me? Why do you keep taking my loved ones, all my father figures?"

If by now you're not able to tell, I did not play about my grandfather. In his eyes, his only grandson did no wrong. He saved me from many beatings by my grandmother. He was so optimistic about everyone's situation. He always saw the good in people and felt there was no need for arguments, disagreements, using foul language, and things of that sort. Just leave it up to my grandfather. He would make it right. He always did. I mean, he was the best grandfather the world had to offer.

To my great-grandfather, my father, and grandfather, as I close this chapter with tears in my eyes, I just wanted the world to know who you guys were, what you meant to me, and how amazing you guys were.

"This too much pain to be living just to die"

— Rod Wave.

CHAPTER
4
TEENAGE FEVER

"**O**h, you think you're grown now?"

"Why yes, yes, I do. Thanks for asking, by the way."

That's what most teenagers would say when they disagree with their parents mumbling those lines under their breath. One thing is for certain, and two things are for sure. First, it's impossible to become an adult without going through those teenage years. Do you know the part of your life where you often become a little secretive from your parents? You don't want the mushy moments from your parents anymore. That would excite you as a child, but now as a young teen, those same mushy moments that your parents found to be so adorable slowly becomes embarrassing. Teen years are tricky, and it can sometimes be quite confusing.

Due to various circumstances, some kids are put into positions to grow up faster than the friends they go to school with every day. That was me. I was one of those kids, not because my family was struggling financially, but because I didn't have anyone left to mold me into becoming the man everyone inspires me to be like as an adult. I didn't have a Denzel Washington, someone who reads black excellence every time he takes a breath of fresh air. I didn't have someone like Russell Wilson, who got drafted in 2012 to the Seattle Seahawks, or even Kobe Bryant, who was drafted in 1996 to the Charlotte Hornets, or Jay-Z, Shawn Corey Carter, a musical icon and even better business genius if there was no father figure around to show me the ropes. I lost everyone who could've done that for me in middle and high school. My uncle (my mom's brother) was still living, but he was off doing Army things and stationed overseas in Germany at the time. Besides, he had his own family to raise anyway, right? My future did not look too good if I needed a male figure. It always crossed my mind-- what life would be like if I decided to give up on myself in those teenage years when I felt like I lost everyone who meant the most to me. How different would things be, or even how strong I had to be to keep going without that manly love or father figure bond I was crying out for at the time? I mean, every adult only wanted to know one thing at a time. They asked, "What do you want to be when you grow up?" I must've heard it a thousand times, at school from teachers, at church, and even from my family.

"Well, guys, I don't know. Please stop with the silly question. I'm still trying to pick up the pieces of my heart that repeatedly shattered if you don't mind."

I thought this was what I wanted to say, but instead, I would randomly blurt out something like an NBA Basketball player.

During my first year in high school, summer basketball camp was where everyone who wanted to try out for the junior varsity team would be. I wore all-black Converse Chuck Taylor's on the first day of practice! Why? Because I was a huge Lil Wayne fan, he made skinny jeans and Converse Chuck Taylor's very popular back then. Now I don't know what decision was worse; wearing converse to tryouts or thinking I could play basketball and try out. It was the natural thing for kids to do; to want to participate in all the sports and be with their friends. My friends probably should have told me basketball was just not "it" for me.

We would face other teams in the Summer Camp Basketball Jamboree games before school and the season started. I rode the bench faithfully with minimal playing time. I only remember getting lucky once as the shot clock was drifting down, and the ball somehow ended up in my hands. What do I do? Awe, what the heck, throw up a shot from the three-point line, and what do you know? It bounces off the backboard and goes in! I remember thinking to myself after the game, that one play, that one shot coach will remember, and that would be enough to make the team.

By this time, tryouts were over, and school had started. Not only was this guy the basketball coach, but he also worked at the school as a teacher and would call those who attended tryouts to his classroom individually to identify who made the team. It was my turn. I was up next, and my heart was beating uncontrollably fast. I have to make the team, or I would definitely be the laughingstock for my friends, and you might've already guessed it from the first day of practice when I told you I wore my all-black converse to practice. I did not make the team. He insulted my intelligence at the time by telling me to try again next year! "What? Try again next year?" I even asked if there was anything else I could do to make the team. What went wrong? I wasn't that bad, was I? He insisted that I wasn't the worst but was not the best. I wanted to slap the stack of papers he had yet to grade for his class off the desk onto the floor. If I did that, I knew I would face more problems.

"So Mack, what did the coach say? Did you make the team?" My friends asked.

Of course, I tried to fabricate the truth. I tried making excuses like, "No, I didn't. But the coach said I was good and he could only have a certain number of players on the team. So, he would have picked me if he could have space for one more person."

Maybe I said something like that or, "The position I was trying for was also what everyone else wanted."

Either way, it was far from the truth. They paused with awkward silence, and I thought, "Okay, maybe they bought that. Not making the team wasn't too bad after all." Then, I heard a slight snicker from my friends, then another, until everyone burst into tears and thought it was the funniest thing in the world. I'll never forget it. Then, the jokes began; my friends were screaming cut! Cut! Cut! They moved their hands in the shape of a scissor cutting an object. I remember getting home and getting off the school bus to see my great-grandmother. My cousin, who made the team mom asked whether I made the team.

Simply replying no, his mom, aunt, and a few others thought this was the funniest thing in the world, and so my visit to my great-grandmother's house got cut short, holding my head down while walking out the door. Strangely it was just a junior varsity basketball team, but why did I feel so hurt inside, so down? Was it that serious? Well, at the time, HELL YES! Coming from where I come from in the hood, the only way out was being one of two things a basketball or football star, at least we thought anyway, and basketball was ruled out for me very early on in my life. So, because it looked like my chances of being someone successful were getting slimmer, I thought the deck was stacked against me. Back then, I might've weighed 125-127 pounds standing at about 5'2. Having meat on my bones and being tall was never really my thing in high school. Being tall will never be my thing. Being 5'6, and a quarter is it for me. Yes, I need my quarter of an inch. Everything counts with your shoes off.

Despite being the laughingstock for about a week, and every time I linked with my friends in the hallway between class periods, they would still move their hands in the form of scissors screaming cut! I was, in fact, one of the popular kids always. A couple of other guy friends and I would form a crew called "Swish We Balling," giving everyone nicknames. Swish We Balling represented the cool kids. You had to have swag. Every freshman wanted to be a part of Swish We Balling, and crews throughout the nearest towns were becoming very popular even though every crew had a name for a different type of reputation. Some were bad, and some were good if you know what I mean.

The worst thing we did was make a teacher cry, be obnoxious in class, and keep talking, laughing, or making jokes. Unlike other crews known for stealing, fighting, going to juvenile detention centers, and dealing drugs, we were never into getting our hands dirty. We all had heart. Getting our hands dirty was never our thing.

Most of us were pretty smart in school. It didn't matter if we decided to be "class clowns" (what they would call students who misbehaved in class back then). Schoolwork came pretty easy for most of us. It was always easy to make the honor roll or keep good grades. I was always good with numbers. I love social studies and could write a paper just as fast as I could do anything else.

I've always been a fast learner. It doesn't take too long for me to learn how to do something. I'd know how to do it better than the person who showed me.

My dad was big on paying attention to detail, and he showed me this by making me wash his Nissan Maxima with him twice a week every summer I was there. I learned details like spraying the water hose to rinse the soap suds off the car so that it's not going back on the car. It's something like a pattern, but I could show you better than I can tell you. I could always hear my dad telling me to take my time and do it right the first time, paying attention to detail. What did they miss? How could you make it better? I became good at picking up on things, especially numbers. My grandpa always said, "Where there is a will, there is a way." It's amazing how much you can learn from someone quickly while continuing to use those tools as life progresses.

Outside of school, many things were happening around me during our free time. Nickel and dime bags of marijuana had hit the streets of Georgetown, South Carolina, like crack did Harlem, New York, back in the 80s. However, this seems to be a good or pretty cool high compared to the hard drugs that flooded the streets back in the day. My aunt had a pink escort, and hotboxing became popular when people started smoking weed. Hotboxing is where a group of smokers sit in a tightly sealed, secluded area and smoke their lungs away, getting high as a kite as smoke from the rolled-up blunt fills the air. So, one day I thought it was a bright idea to sit in my aunt's pink Escort while she and her friend's hotbox. Sitting there was the second worse decision I had made in weeks, entering my first year of high school. I found out quickly what was the meaning of "hotbox."

Let me tell you another story inside of a story. I sat inside my aunt's Escort while they passed the blunt around. It seemed normal at first. I mean, it's just smoke. Before I knew it, everything became hilarious. I was laughing at everything under the sun. Apparently, I was just hit with a boost of laughing gas. My cousins were all trying to figure out what was funny, as my aunt smiled and laughed, saying, "He's got contact."

Now, of course, at the time, I was not a smoker. I didn't know what a contact high was. It was defined as getting high from the smoke or "good gas" that floats around in the air. The smoke is still entering your lungs because you're breathing it in.

So, you mean to tell me I was, in fact, high without actually smoking or putting my lips to a blunt through catching contact? As the hotboxing session went on, I became dramatically hot, with sweat dripping down my chest and my face. I needed to get out of there. I couldn't take it anymore. I felt like I was going to die. They all responded NO! They said I would break the hotbox by letting the doors open or rolling the windows down. I waited a few minutes and tried to roll down the window to climb out with my shirt off, eventually bursting out the door for a breath of fresh air. I mean, you should've seen it. Imagine someone waking up, not just up; I'm talking about the one where you jump out of your sleep expeditiously, sitting up in bed before realizing everything is alright. That was me. It's almost like I came back to life when the fresh outside air breached my face again. Let me tell you; they were so upset they screamed. I was never to hotbox again with them. They said, If you can't take the pressure, don't turn up the stove!

I did not plan on it anyway.

I mean, what was so special about getting high anyway. Now, let me be honest. I never said I did not try smoking a couple of times to see what it was like. Overall, it was not for me. I also didn't drink at the time.

I remember being in Andrews, South Carolina, with my dad's side of the family and my cousin. I always ran with guys a few years older than us, so it was too easy to get someone at the nearest corner store or gas station of age to buy you a small bottle of liquor. At the time, Mad Dog 20/20 and Wild Rose were what we had. They are both still around. We also liked "bootleggers," which were different name-brand liquors on hand. Unfortunately, it did not matter if a baby walked up to the door; as long as the money was green, they would sell it to you.

Man, what were we thinking, just drinking anything to say we were doing it? It had to be a Friday or Saturday night because every weekend, I mostly spent in Andrews with my dad's side of the family. One night, we were making our rounds, ready to get drunk, and some of our friends had a treehouse built behind their house — I mean, an actual tree. We discovered they were sipping on a new drink called Four Loko— eight to fourteen percent alcohol content with every flavor you could think of; Watermelon, Apple, Grape, Peach, Lemonade, Mango, you name it. This stuff tasted amazing, and it was only right that we all retreated to the store to buy our can. This particular night stuck with me. I purchased the lemonade flavor and was ready to hang out for the night. It was so easy to drink. I mean, was alcohol even in this thing like the can ads? I couldn't taste a thing, so what did I do? I kept chugging away. It tasted delicious, just like juice, and eventually, I figured out that was the trick behind the drink. It tasted good, but that's not all it had for you. After finishing my tall 23.5oz 695ml can, it did not take long for me to start feeling different. I remember trying to stand up to walk and falling back down to the couch because my legs were gone. I couldn't feel them. Everything from the waist down felt like complete Jello. My head was pounding, and my eyes began playing tricks on me like I was just picked up and spun around fifty times until I was dizzy.

My stomach was doing the royal rumble and hitting me with three-piece combinations like Floyd Money Mayweather, and I was beginning to feel bad. My body did not like this Four Loko drink. Somehow, I managed to hang over the toilet on my knees, making the silly noises you make when you're trying to throw up, but nothing came out except liquid fluids here and t ere. Come to think of it, throwing up almost sounds like a car with a bad ignition. It won't fire up, so instead, it returns a random noise. Was that it? Had I drunk on an empty stomach with nothing to soak up the alcohol? How was I supposed to know? I was maybe fourteen at the time.

I didn't have any business drinking anyway. An empty stomach on top of an upset stomach and pounding headache is a terrible feeling. Who's with me? Who's been on that bathroom floor on their knees, crotched over the toilet, begging God to take this feeling away? I promise you I won't ever drink no more! Please, God, take it away. Isn't it funny how when we're in tough or sticky situations is when most of us look to pray or call on the higher power? That was very much so me back then. I was wasted. Eventually, my cousin and older guys we hung out with gave me some water and bread and a couple of different things to eat to put stuff on my stomach, and I was returning to life yet again, having to save myself. This was rough. If drinking felt like that, I also wanted no parts, and I mean it. It's not like I was nowhere even close to being legal to drink regardless r right. Yea, being intoxicated or high just wasn't for me. The idea of a substance being able to take control of me and my thoughts mentally also my body physically just wasn't a good look if you abused the substance. I mean, it's not like a fourteen-year-old is supposed to be aware of his tolerance level at that age. We just knew to drink until the bottle or can was empty, and the result of what you get is what you got.

By now, you have probably realized that my dad and mom were from two different parts of South Carolina; not far distance-wise at all from each other, maybe 20 minutes or so, but still from two different areas.

This brings me to my story about the summer before starting tenth grade. I and my right-hand man name Snakehead, were in Andrews, South Carolina. Not my dad's neck of the woods, but an area called Italy. We were probably visiting the Bootlegger late that night to get some liquor and drink. Regardless at this point in our life, the generations before us had already made their mark, and things were getting worse.

It was not wise to be in different places or territories you shouldn't, like being in Andrews when you were really from the country (Route 4). Now, in some parts of Andrews, my dad was from there, so I got a pass in places like C-City (Crossroad) and Deerwood, and that was about it. Uptown and West Hell. When they found out that I was B.G.'s nephew, I most likely was hated, even though my uncle was fresh into his prison sentence, serving what looked like life at the time. It didn't matter. He still had enemies, which meant his kids and family did too. Not to make it any better, a well-known popular guy had got shot and died uptown before my uncle got booked, and members from West Hell believed he was the guy who ordered the hit. Now even though, to my knowledge, this was not true, it didn't matter. They wanted someone to pay. My uncle was from Baltimore, so he and his brothers and their soldiers knew what time it was.

Whatever was going to happen would eventually happen.

Snakehead and I were walking late one night in Italy, just looking for anything to get into, and suddenly, he pulled out something that appeared to be shiny and chrome at the time. There it was, his grandpa's chrome 22. She was a beauty! I instantly wanted to flip it over a couple of times. It was already cocked with one round in the chamber and ready to let it rip. The adrenalin suddenly came over me, and before you knew it, I raised my arm upper ward pointing towards the sky, and let a few rounds off. "ANG! ANG! ANG! Yeaaaaa," we both said while continuously walking and laughing before his sister returned to take us home. It was something about your first time toting that iron back then that made me feel different. "I've got to get myself one!" It wasn't even the thought of how dangerous this could be for kids at fourteen and fifteen walking around with guns and how much trouble we could get into if things went wrong. I don't think that Snake cared much about that anyway. He always said, "Mack, it wasn't faking with this shit." He said that with a straight face. Not that he was necessarily going out looking for trouble, but he wasn't ducking it or turning his head away, either.

He stood on principle and lived up to it in every fight and altercation. That's just what he believed as he was slowly but surely turning to the streets. Whatever came with that, he was down for it, and best believe toting that 22 if it ever came down to it, fifteen years old or not, he wasn't bluffing, and it wasn't for shits and giggles.

See, coming from where we come from, the majority of us had developed this same similar concept in life and had already been through a lot being in a low-income poverty area. "Whatever it was going to be was just that. There was no running. You just have to do whatever it is your thinking to me. However, it went is just what we would have to live or die with".

This was a crazy concept to live by. Being in the hood and having heart is what made you a man, and that's all we knew at the time.

By the time our tenth-grade year had started, things were getting out of control, and the streets were taking our country by storm. Every football and basketball game led to a shooting or fight at the end. Every teen party was being shut down because crews were fighting. The funniest thing about this situation is that we were a country. Our biggest rivalries were Georgetown, our nearest city. We hated each other. Why? I have no clue this war started before my time before I was born, which trickled down through generations from my uncle (my mother's brother) on his own. What made this funny was discovering the country had nothing; we had to go into town to get things like fast food, gas, the nearest Walmart, the courthouse, and anything we needed. Did this matter? Not. Wherever we saw the enemy, or the enemy saw us, it was going down. Think of these turfs in the shape of a triangle Georgetown, Route 4, and Andrews, except for a few others who eventually got involved in Hemingway and Myrtle Beach.

I'll never forget the day we were sitting in math class, and one of my friends said, "Man, what do you think about joining a gang, being a Blood? I didn't know how to respond. We weren't known for having gangs where I'm from, like Crips or Bloods. We had crews repping where they were from. Gangs were beginning to grow in the area. He said that he had been asked to join a gang and become a Blood being bounty hunter "come home" is what they called it, but he wasn't sure at the time. If he was going to say yes, he had to fight a few guys after school once we all made it home. Long story short, the next day, he, sure enough, had a few bruises but, most importantly, his red flag on him, and must I had it could do those things with his fingers well (stacking). Well, "that was quick," I thought, but then he eventually was all in with the streets doing heavy drugs and popping pills, and things sort of went downhill from there for his life, which was unfortunate. I guarantee his gang probably never knew how smart he was in school, especially in math, I was good, but he was better. We would battle to see who could get the highest scores on pop quizzes and tests. Then, two months into my tenth-grade year, something else changed my life forever. Yet, another permanent scar. I would find myself in the middle of when the most fun was taking place for me, and we were finally growing up as teens in the back seat of my mom's charcoal grey Tahoe with all my things packed and heading north to Fort Drum, New York, right outside of a little town called Water town.

I lived about 30 minutes from Canada, and things quickly became a nightmare. I was afraid I wouldn't fit in or that this southern boy would freeze to death. Either way, I wasn't going to make it up here and wanted to go home back to South Carolina. My grandmother (my mother's mom) had this bright idea that my mom was fresh off her deployment, and it was time I moved up to New York with her. She was getting up in age, and to be honest. I was probably driving her up the wall with a nervous breakdown every time I left the house to hang out. You know elders have their spider senses. Once you've reached a certain age, you automatically gain the right to say, "You can't fool me. I've been there and done that." Where I'm from, my elders ran that saying in the hole.

News traveled like clockwork in the hood, so the house phone at the time was the best thing ever created for elders. They would be on the phone gossiping for hours, talking about who died, who just got locked up, what they did, and who said what in church this past Sunday. So, my grandma was no stranger to what was going on outside. She was hip, for sure. She had this dramatic story about how the streets would take me over and watched the colors I would wear to school, declaring I was in a gang or getting ready to join one. The days when I may have had just a glimpse of red in my clothing or wearing a red shirt, she just knew I was a Blood.

I had a few fights and a couple of suspensions for being too talkative in class, talking back here and there to teachers, but other than that being a troublemaker or going to put me in unwise situations was never my style. By tenth grade, I was pretty popular and went to school with money in my pocket. So, it was nothing for me to go to school with a hundred dollars in a few twenties, a couple of fifty-dollar bills, and one big blue face hundred-dollar bill totaling anywhere from about three hundred to a little over five hundred dollars. I was fly with the latest gear at the school was never so bad for me, and I enjoyed learning. All subjects were alright in my book. Now, I never really maintained all A's. It was more of a mixture of A's and B's, then occasionally falling off to a C. Getting bad grades was never cool to me, and I'm sure I could've maintained all A's if I wanted to. So, that's the story of how I left South Carolina and ended up in Watertown, New York. Now, if I did not know any better at the time, I thought this was the worse decision possible, but in return, it landed me another permanent scar, but this one slowly became a positive.

On my first day of school, I was dramatic at its finest. Would I fit in? Would all eyes be on me like Tupac?

Indian River High School was my first culture shock. Why? Because I was no longer going to Carver's Bay Bears high school, which averaged around 350 students per year, and about 300 of us were probably black. No, this time, it was different, and the school was even bigger at Indian River, averaging over 800 students per year. Not everyone looked like me. There were various ethnicities, different cultures, many different backgrounds, and walks of life. The exciting news was on my first day. No one acted like they saw a ghost. I fitted right in, and before you knew it, within my first week,

I was running with another crew. They were military kids from the Carolinas and Georgia, so we were all trying to stick together as this was new to us.

Indian River is where I discovered German for learning my second language. I instantly thought, wow, we for sure have nothing like this at the school I went to back home. I mean, the whole format of school schedules and the subjects were different. I went from sitting in one class period for over an hour and getting out of school at around three o'clock to moving up north, and by the time 2 O'clock rolled around, the school was over, and the class periods weren't long at all, maybe what seemed like forty-five min test. One thing remained the same to me no matter what school I went to; the lunch was never good. No matter the school, the state, or the area. I told my mom I needed to take my lunch to school, or I would die of starvation from not eating all day, and you don't want your only son (at the time) to die. So, she fell for it, and I had my lunch going to school at the time, which come to think of it, wasn't much of nothing either, packed inside of a brown paper bag, my favorite which was a peanut butter only sandwich No jelly! I absolutely hate jelly. To someone who may read this one day, you didn't think I only ate those famous peanut butter sandwiches as a young child, did you? That's right there, here to stay. My peanut butter-only sandwich was cut horizontally into two triangles, Nacho cheese Doritos or Cool Original, a bag of fruit snacks, and a Capri Sun. I thought this was a delicious meal to die for.

By this time, I was into the swing of things and had friends hanging out, and New York was not so bad after all; cold, very cold, freezing actually during the fall and winter months, but yes, it wasn't so bad after all. Except, Yea theirs always an except. Things weren't just going to keep going my way. There I was on the first day of football practice. The quarterback calls "Hut," and I take the ball and run it right up the middle and score on the practice defense untouched, smoking everyone in a foot race to the endzone because I was the next best fastest thing close to lighting you now. Well, My first day of practice went nothing like that. It went the complete opposite. The quarterback hikes the ball, and I take the handoff up the middle. I was stuffed right at the line.

I met my match plied right at the line of scrimmage; come on, guys, the coach blows the whistle while yelling at the O-line for not bloc ing. There I was under the pile and in pain, now if you happened to miss my weight previously, around my tenth-grade year, I was a buck 25, maybe somewhere up in there, and the O-linemen had fallen on my ankle, leaving me lining in an awkward position and these were some big boys. My ankle felt crushed; I didn't know, rather scream for help calling out, "Maaaa!" I mean, you should've seen it; it was swelling so fast it looked like someone had stuffed two red apples in ide. I did know; however, a very short-lived season was ending quickly, at least for a few weeks per app. I couldn't walk, and the practice field was far away from the high school building locker room. Now my friends are holding me up while I'm hopping back on one leg with many rest breaks in between, of course, until we finally made it back. The next day my mom took me to the doctor's office, and as we imagined, it wasn't broken, but it sure was a bad ankle sprain and bruised up pretty badly.

As the Doctor said, "you'll be on crutches for a few weeks, then a follow-up appointment leading into a brace, granted everything is healing properly." I looked at my mom with a blink steer, crutches!? At that moment, I was very judgmental about crutches, and the thought of having them was not sitting right with me. It took some getting used to, but boy was I wrong; now, if you've never been on crutches for a couple of weeks, then maybe you should do something to try it out. My judgment on crutches was incorrect. It wasn't so bad. It was pretty nice. It was like my teenage mini vacation for not having to carry my books around school, grab my lunch, or perhaps be expected to do much of anything compliments from my friends, and of course, I took advantage o it. Yup, that's right, my mom wasn't calling me out of the room to grab her the remote off the table because she was comfortably lying on the couch and could've just got up and got it her elf. Didn't you hate that as a teenager? Whose parent has ever called you out of your room to do something so simple for them while thinking in your head, "Wowwww, really, mom, you honestly could've just done that yourself!" But of course, it's your parents, so you do it anyway. No, taking out the trash for a couple of weeks, and I was taking full advantage of this opportunity, and now I was the one doing the calling to hand me the remote off the table because it was too painful to move.

Yes, finally! Payback! Eventually, my right ankle was back to its usual self, and my mom was coming down on orders for Fort Lewis, Washington. Now before we go any further, I must add that I had no idea Washington was even a state at this point in my life. All jokes aside, I mean, are we talking about Washington, D.C., where we're at least a little closer back to South Carolina? Because the truth was, I did adapt to New York in the case that month or two, but I was still homesick and missing my childhood friends. No, jokes, my mom said Fort Lewis is in Washington state.

"Didn't you know Washington was a state?"

"No, I did not, actually, but thank you. I'm just now learning middle of my tenth-grade year that Washington is a state. So, what do I do next?"

"Well, what would anyone else do that did not know that Washington was a state? Pull up a map!"

"Of course!"

And, low and behold, Washington was a state. The tiptoe left-hand corner of the United States of America resides in Washington.

"But wait, how were we supposed to get there? Fly? But I've never flown before, and I'm not sure if it was out of fear or simply because I had never been anywhere that caused me to fly there."

"No, silly. We're going to drive there," she said.

I replied, "Drive, mom? Seriously? Do you see how many states are over there? It'll take us forever to get there."

"It's only forty-two hours and two thousand eight hundred fifteen miles, to be exact."

I guess it's true what they say, "Beggers cannot be choosers." I had never flown before, so that was out of the question, and we could not walk there, so driving was the only option. Then, as you can imagine, after the military came and packed up our home, one of the perks about being in the military, on top of traveling, your home was packed and shipped to your next destination free of ch page. Now, I did not say that things didn't possibly get banged up or broken along the way, but your house whole goods got t ere. After a few months of residing in New York, I was off to the races again, sitting in the back of that charcoal grey Chevy Tahoe leaving another group of friends and my newfound favorite German tea here. You know, the movies where the kid moves from his neighborhood, and all his friends are standing outside watching. They begin to run behind the car until there out of breath and cannot keep up anymore as the little boy or girl looks out the back window at their friends with sad puppy expressions. That's exactly what I felt was happening, uncontrollable emotions of moving yet again in a matter of months. Of course, none of my friends were chasing the car down, screaming bye Markus, but that was my imagination of the movies and what I felt was taking place. "The Army doesn't care that I have friends," I would think to myself. I'm never joining the Army. All my mother do is work, I would repeat to myself". Yes, I was wrong about not joining the military, but soon enough, you'll find that out. It only took us forever and a day to finally get to Washington, our new home, and on this trip, I discovered two of the NGS. First, mountains are real, and it could be a beautiful sight to see besides your hair popping as you adjust to the different altitudes going up and down, in and out of the mountains. Number two, I was, in fact, still motion sickness from car rides. I could never ride in a car for long periods of hours at a time without getting motion sickness, overheating, and throwing up.

I remember traveling back home to South Carolina from Fort Stewart, Georgia, with my nana and family after just attending my dad's military funeral and overheating so severely in the car I began to throw up. We had to pull over on the side of the road. It wasn't good. Motion sickness inside a vehicle for long periods would get me every time; a few hours was all it took. I had just lost my father now I was throwing up all over myself.

There I was, finally arriving in Washington state and going through Seattle, and my mom pointed and said," Look, so that's the space needle!"

"Wow, that's cool. What are they doing up there?"

"It's an observation deck and a rotating restaurant."

"So, they have a restaurant high up in the air like that? That's so cool."

I lived in Washington state for almost three years and never ate at the Space Needle. So, we arrived in Lacey, Washington North Thurston County, to be exact, Balustrade Blvd in the Horizon Pointe community. It wasn't hard to tell that I was not on the east coast or down south anymore. I was, however, many miles away from South Carolina, and you could tell. My mother and stepdad had outdone themselves with this one. I mean, the neighborhood was amazing. The homes in Horizon Pointe were astonishing, and I remember being amazed and everything I saw; There isn't anything like the suburbs where I've lived. Everyone was living their absolute best life in the neighborhood, walking their dawgs, taking morning and nightly jogs; there was a huge recreation park with a football field and a full-court basketball gym, and get this; the goal nets were all still in the full act. No paintings, graffiti writing on the backboards, no run-down equipment. The kids out here had it made.

"What school am I going to?" I asked mom. She replied, "Timberline Blazers High school."

The following day came, and we headed for school. I remember arriving out front and asking if this was my school; it looked more like a college campus. Everything out here is big and triple times the size of what I'm used to. Could you imagine going from a school with a little over three hundred fifty students to about eight students, then suddenly, you're at a mini college campus with over sixteen hundred students, is that culture shock at its finest or what? I remember the principal going over some of the guidelines and policies of the school; he was a much older guy and had been doing this for a while. He made points such as Timberline High School was an open campus; wait, what?!

What is an open campus, sir? He chuckled and began explaining to me that due to various circumstances, for one, some kids did not have a full day schedule at school some only had a few classes, so they possibly only would have to come to school a little before noon or come in early and leave early due to doubling up on classes, advancing a grade which would put them early in graduating. Therefore, you could pretty much come and go as you please, and for lunch, most kids with cars they and their friends went had lunch at the nearest fast-food restaurants or just went home for lunch.

My neighborhood was only about ten minutes from the school, not far at all. Kids would skateboard, walk, drive, and ride the bus, all sorts of ways to get to school. I was smiling from ear to ear at this point, and my mom facial expression looked like it was saying, "Don't get any ideas." Timberline was surrounded by what I would call nice neighborhoods for the most part. The principal explained that cell phones, hats, and such were permitted as long as it wasn't disruptive in class or during the study. This was a good life. If all schools were like this, maybe I would enjoy going more, and before moving any further, I would, without a doubt, presume that based on this first conversation with my principal at Timberline High School, I quickly learned that every place in the world was not the same. Here it seemed as though you were being treated as a young adult, and it was up to you to mess those privileges up; the majority of the population had no idea of the world I came from, so what they were used to I just wasn't. If you've ever been to the west coast and live on the east coast down south, everything is night and day; a clear difference once. The swag, the vocabulary, the music, the houses, the food, it's just completely different. A hood or the projects in South Carolina is nothing like what was being called the hood in Washington, they were still pretty nice homes to me, and of course, things went on, but I guess it just wasn't up close in my face as of what I was use too. Come to think of it, I'm not sure I never recalled seeing a single or double-wide trailer in the area we lived in, but I'm sure I could find them if I looked hard enough; the state is pretty big. Its real gangs are a huge culture out west, and Crips were well known along with Bloods. I would say more Crips were in that area. Even still, they were gangsters but just regular people. When I saw my first rolling 60 crips screaming neighborhood on the set, I expected them to be rough around the edges, deep into the hard knock's life, and serious all the time with a scary-looking face and mean-mugging. Maybe that stereotype is true for some, but the crips I knew were cool. They laughed and joked just like everyone else. They were normal and quite intelligent in school to add the same for the bloods. It's not always that they were looking for trouble or out to harm someone from the other side or anyone who was not a part of their set. They just lived by a different set of rules, their code as what was seen as their family. As long as you didn't disrespect or cross those lines, you were fine, but again, even though I've always had friends that became members of the rolling 60s and blood nothing against it, it was never for me or my style of doing things. Now, off to my first day of school, I can vividly remember what I should wear; I can wear hats my fake chains; WowWee, I'm about to be fresh to death! I'm looking in my bathroom mirror, pacing back and forth from my closet. So, I threw on my blue and orange Chicago bear hat with the embroidery of my name on the side (By the way, hats were my thing back then, I had so many hats that I eventually started selling them for $20 each. I guess you could say I was a Hustler before I knew what a Hustler was. That lesson my dad had taught me years beforehand at the dollar store would stick with me forever and never leave my mind. If I did not understand anything else, I understood the value of a dollar and how to get it). Now back to what I was wearing on my first day, looking so fresh and so clean with a new pair of 501 slim fit Levi jeans to add a polo shirt, and some Jordan 4's like the colorway of the retro Cav 4's that were released two years later in 2012 that were black, orange, and blue and we cannot forget the fake chain that had the orange Kool-Aid character pendant on it like the rapper OJ The Juiceman chain he would always wear in his music vi eos. Yea, that was it. I'm ready for my first day now with a fresh dreadlock t ist. Yes, yes, yes to someone who made me read this one day. I had dreads in high school, which got pretty long to the length of my chest. My first day was different, I was now the minority, but that was okay because I could honestly say that even with my first day of school, I was always accepted as I was. I have never experienced any racist altercation; I could fill this book with various scenarios where Caucasians helped me over my skin color if that was the topic.

On my first day of school, things were moving so fast; it would take me forever to learn where my classes were, and I lost count of how many times I got lost. I mean, a school with three levels, it seemed like it went up, down, and around then down again to include a lower basement-type level with classes. That's right, the A, B, and C wings are what it was called.

Finally, making it over to A.P. statistics, I remember taking an empty seat. Then, as the class went on, the conversation sparked because of my fake Kool-Aid pendant chain; hey, what's that? I explained what it was, and from there, the icebreaker was set. I was the new kid on the block, and everyone took a liking to it; maybe it was because everything about me screamed southern down to my Geechee accent that I eventually would lose in the years to come. Just like what I had imagined for them, it was the same on their end, nothing they had ever seen in her. I was talking well to them, and I was talking way too fast and not pronouncing my words fully. Did you say skreet or street? I had never heard so many "highs" and "what does that mean" in my life. Later that week, I would find myself in the library, perhaps on the computer or searching for a book. The library, of course, was a decent size upstairs; I would come across one of my high school best friends in Washington. Soon as he spoke to introduce himself, I could tell he wasn't from around here. He was straight out of Mississippi, only here in Washington because his stepmother had recently gotten stationed there. It was a good bit of the population that were military kids, so we all knew what it was like always having to move, adjust and meet new people.

His older brother, his little sister, and he all went to Timberline, and I would find out that we all lived a few houses down from each of her. This would work out perfectly, his older brother had the new dodge challenger, and that's who I would begin riding to and from school with. We would later form a crew called TMT (The Money Team). We thought we were Floyd Money Mayweather and his crew or something. It didn't take long for me to get adjusted, and unlike New York, I loved every bit of Washington. A lot of my friends were Samoan, and I began to learn their culture as well and loved it. I thought I was a huge white rice eater, but they loved white rice also like love it. For the years I attended Timberline, my second half of tenth-grade year up until my senior graduation, we were always pretty good at everything, Football, Basketball, Track, Tennis, Volleyball, Swimming (yes, my school had a swimming pool, and it was so cool), Baseball, Volleyball you name it being a 4A school. We were well-rounded in sports.

There was a girl who played basketball, and her life was surrounded by it. She was ranked nationally. I'm talking about how she had a game. I mean, serious game. Guys would not even play her, or she would end up embarrassing them. For varsity game warmups, she would go around the three-point line from one side to the other, shooting three-pointers, and eventually, the other team we were facing would stop and stare at her. She was that good. She would eventually go on to New Mexico on a full-ride scholarship leading them to their first NCAA Tournament since 1988 with 73 three-pointers made that season, making her the number 2 all-time Aggie. Just heading into her senior year, she had accumulated 191 three-pointers made. When it was all said and done, she was top 20 in the scoring of all time as an Aggie and played in the All-WAC first-team tournament, then became the WAC All-Academic member for consecutive seasons. Everyone knew she would graduate and go off to live up to the hype. My best friend's brother was the fastest in the school with a set of track spikes on and would also go off to run in some of the big Oregon Duck meets against De'Anthony Thomas and now plays for the Kansas City Chefs. Our quarterback was also special, traveling to make combines and play in All-American Bowls in Texas. This school was no stranger to athletes, as most would go off to continue their careers in sports. Our head coach was huge on recruiting and getting his players to the next level, and it seemed like he knew all the right people. Once my best friend's brother graduated, I was officially the fastest person in the school, and that's why I became known for being fast. Besides, it wasn't too hard to pinpoint me anyway. My dreads were long, and I would dye the tips red orange. Please don't ask why it was popular. I wanted to do what I saw on T.V., and everyone around the school would say they reminded them of hot Che too. The field and track became my peace. We had the finest equipment and a friendly gym with many coaches. The school was a piece of cake. Why? Because, again, I never acted out in school for the most part, except for this one time a kid came from another school right before me, and the football team was about to hit the weight room to get started for football practice. Would you believe he showed up? Word around town had gotten out that the kid had a problem with me, you know, typical playa hating, and that was the news all day at school, so I had already told my mom and stepdad if he did show up, what was going to happen so be expected to pick me up from school and my step dad replied handle your business so from there that was my cue if anything was going to go down take my business.

I was stretching, but suddenly we began to hear a clap of thunder, and people were screaming, but in excitement, as if something was about to go down and it was getting louder and closer. Upon arriving at the gym door, it was him. Before I knew it, off instinct, I ran to the door and blacked out before any words could be exchanged. I caught him with a combination two-piece, and the rest was history. I remember picking him up by the legs, and somehow we were near a trashcan. I didn't realize it at the time, but when I threw him over, he went inside, which was the highlight of the fight. I don't remember much after that, but I was always calm and just remembered my stepdad asking the principal why I had to be suspended if a kid from a whole other school came to fight me and started it. The principal did not want to, but it was a part of the protocol. I'm guessing I sat home for a few days and remember my stepdad cracking jokes about me being out here beating up pe ple. My mother, I don't recall her saying much about it. The worse part about this was I was missing a game Friday night lights. I eventually returned to school and received praise from everyone. My popularity was at an all-time high, and they knew what the south was about. The guy I fought cousin even found me on Facebook and wrote me telling me that I had to earn their respect. They were in a gang, but I was alright with them. Even at school, I would receive notes and study material from classmates they had made for me while I missed a few days because, as mentioned, school subjects were not hard for me, and I liked learning, so they did me justice there without even me as ing. My high school consisted of me mainly keeping good grades, attending combines for sports, traveling for track meets and championships, and playing foot. I tried working for a summer once at goodwill. Our quarterback mother was the hiring manager, but once school started, my mother thought it was a good idea to focus on sports. She didn't want me getting off late at night after attending football or track practice according to the season we were in (as you can see, I never tried out for basketball again), then having to repeat that daily would eventually take a toll on me.

I would have had to give something up. Colleges up and down the west coast were sending campus invites and letters, so she thought I should focus on sp rts. My weekends would consist of hitting the lake with my friends, and it would be packed. This was the hang-out spot at the lake for the summer and big bonfire outings for the winter, and although my friends would dive off the docks, I never did trust it, so I never actually got in the water. After that, we would come back, freshen up and support a few of our friends who played R by. Now, I never got into it because the sport looked a little too rough for my liking, and I would always imagine myself breaking my kneecap, but I enjoyed watching my friends play, and their team was pretty good around the city. I had a lot of first-time experiences in Washington, being introduced to Rugby and sitting lakeside; my first time eating Panda Express was one day for school lunch when my friends decided that we were going to panda for lunch, and of course, I was clueless while asking what's hat?

They all yelled, "OMG! YOU'VE NEVER HAD PANDA EXPRESS?!"

"Ugh! No, I haven't." I replied. "They don't have that where I'm from."

And they got excited, replying, "Oh, we're about to put you on, bro!" And ever since that day, I fell in love. It was something about that grilled chicken teriyaki back then that clinched my appetite every single time. Lacey, Washington, is also where I got introduced to a kickback. I always asked, "what's that" about something I didn't know. Our crew was all famous and was known for sports, so of course, we were always invited. I had white friends, Black, Hispanic, Native, and Samoan. You name it, our crew was pretty versatile, so we fit in with everyone.

A kickback was a house party, and Friday and Saturday nights off would go. This was the next best thing to the movie Project X. And, where are your parents always throwing these huge house parties in these nice big homes? One thing about a west coast kickback is it wasn't a real kickback if you couldn't smell the aroma in the air smacking your face soon as you stepped foot through the front door or the garage. Yes, indeed, I was never a smoker, but the West Coast has the best marijuana or, should I say, gas. I mean, the aroma would fill the air smelling just right, setting a mood to catch a good vibe to set the tone of the night. At the kickbacks, they blew down but with bongs and not your typical blunt that I was used to seeing down south. I got my license here and the same week got into a fender bender. I mean, could you blame me? What's the purpose of a roundabout, whose bright idea was to put those things in the middle of the road and get this? It was my friend's parent's car because he did not have his license yet. Well, you guessed it, that was embarrassing, and I felt like my life was over. Come to think of it, it was only a fender bender, and I exaggerated the situation. No one was even mad, and my mother took care of it.

How about another story inside of a story? The football team decided we would have some fun this weekend and go egging. Yes, I can tell it now. It was our famous quarterback idea, and if we ever egged your car around town, I'm apologizing for us all right here right now! Hopefully, it didn't scratch the paint of your guys' nice ride, but what the heck? We were still teens at the end of the day, right, and trouble would at least find you occasionally. So, there we're one Saturday night after, purchasing bulk loads of eggs from a popular grocery store out in Washington called Safeway. Remember all those nice neighborhoods I was telling you about? Well, one neighborhood would have a woods forest type behind it with a trail that would lead to the main highway, a well-traveled road.

For our hours were throwing eggs from the woods and egging cars, but for the most part, they would keep rising, probably not realizing what had happened. One of our friends decided they had had enough of this. We had been out here for hours all night. We were running low on eggs, and it was time to get the reaction we were looking for. He decided that the next car that road by, we could see them coming from a distance, so he left the wood line and ran as close as possible to the car and started unloading eggs out of his hoodie pocket on the car. We all thought you were going to do what?! Long story short, it was not hard to convince us all to go with him. We were a team, and most importantly, like brothers, every Thursday before our games, we would even have dinner at a designated player's house to eat and just bond and build that relationship. We were in, and the car was approaching; I mean, I didn't think anything of it. I knew I was the fastest, so if anything went wrong, it would not have been me getting caught, and no way they were going to dime me outright. The car was getting closer. We ran out, probably scaring the life out of whoever was driving with all of us having on dark clothing, hoodies, and beanies, and unloaded on this car, bringing it to a complete top. I mean, you just had to be there. Could you imagine twenty-plus guys unloading egg after egg on your car around midnight, and you coming from God's knowledge, were?

We were pretty athletic and fit guys working out daily, so the eggs sounded like bullet shots. How hard we were throwing them, and then a car door opened, and we took off. Right here is where things began to get real as my adrenaline, pumping out of my chest, heard a slight cock; now, even though I was only a junior in high school, I was no stranger to guns coming from where I was from. I know what I heard, followed by foul language; you would think this guy was angry or big mad as they would say today. Omg, he's chasing us! We all hit the wood line and scattered; we knew once we made it back to the wood line, we had him beat. No one knew those woods like us.

He stopped while still cursing and yelling at the top of his lungs. We made it back to the other side, exiting out to the neighborhood and heading for our cars, laughing and joking like, man, well, that was fine for ton, right? At least, we thought it was over; this guy had other plans for this group of kids. We see car lights hit the neighborhood as the engine revives, and he's flying, coming towards our direction; he had driven all the way around to the neighborhood. My guy screams, "Ooooh shit!" and takes off now; what do you do when someone you're with takes off run in? Well, run right; you'll find out why they're running later once things are settled and they've stopped. We ran back into the woods and lay down flat on the ground as his lights were circling the block; he noticed the cars as he got out and began just talking recklessly again about how terrible of kids we were, who raised us, and so on. Little did he know we were the Timberline Blazers, football team.

The city loved us, with pictures in every restaurant and newspaper articles every week, and we did volunteer work like cutting elders' grass and washing cars at the school on Saturday mornings. Still, as stated, occasionally, trouble would just fine you. I mean, boys can't be perfect, right? He tried to wait us out with threats and all sorts of other things, but that wasn't going to happen. We could lay in these woods all night, it was a Saturday night, and quite frankly, we had nothing else better to do. He eventually gave up and went about his business; I remember the following Monday sitting in Digital photography, where we had a project to create our website using code, and zoning out thinking, man, I almost died this weekend; that was a close one. I mean, could you imagine the Monday news headline or the high school newspaper headlines, "twenty plus kids of the Timberline high school football are reportedly left dead after a night of egging takes a turn for the left after a raged driver whose car was egged pulls out his gun and starts blasting everyone." Man, that would have devastated our families and the school without a football team. See, even though I had grown to love the environment, I was in.

The people I was around, the expansion of what life was like outside of the hood being in a place like this and going to a school of this caliber where a huge cafeteria was downstairs and then pizza, rice- chicken, ice cream, slushes, candy all of the popular food types was upstairs at the student center available for purchase, but this also meant for bigger risk. Sometimes crazy things did take place; the more people, the bigger the school does not always mean better in every category. I also encountered some heartfelt experiences; kids were bullied, and some even resulted in committing suicide. Now no suicides at my school, but they were at a couple of others in the county. I remember it like yesterday someone hanging themselves behind the sky, which sort of left a black cloud over schools for a w il. We did have a couple of bomb threats at our school where we had to clear the building, but it was hard to get anything past us at Timberline; we were in with the security guard who also somehow was the basketball coach; I mean, he was a security guard, but he was cool as a fan, and everyone was pretty much cool with him, kind of buff black guy who was a sneakerhead and treated his drop like it was a dress contest every day wearing something new. Still, I guess that was his way of fitting in and always knowing "the word around town" and relaying it to us.

One normal day, the school goes on lockdown, and you can hear a helicopter overhead, the hallways are dark, and everyone is locked inside the class. Parents were panicking because, of course, we had phones and updated them on what was going on, but we were not allowed to leave school until the issue was resolved. Well, remember the kid I had fought? His older cousins were out of school and got involved in some mischief, being at the wrong place at the wrong time. When a couple of guys decided to rob another set of guys entered the house, the deal went south, shots rang off, and people died. Don't let the pretty places fool you. It can still go on. Now word has it that he was not at the house but met up with the alleged shooter after the fact. He was never charged with anything some say he told, or should I say snitched, but who knows, that was none of my concern. Unfortunately, a friend of mine was not a close friend or anything, but he was a guy we were cool with, and his little sister, who was in a grade under us, was also popular. Being at the wrong place at the wrong time, he was charged with accessory while his friend received murder, and they're both still serving that same sentence today. It was unfortunate because he was an intelligent young man who graduated school early with flying colors and was an exceptional athlete in basketball. Still, he just got caught up in the streets, and one wrong choice of decisions would cost him his life behind bars. This shook the school, and no one could believe this had happened, but that wouldn't be the only thing that would take a turn for me. It always seemed like when things went left for me, they began to keep going that way, and I could never grasp the steering wheel to pull it back right until it was too far. My mother and stepfather were preparing for deployment to Afghanistan, and I did not want to move back to South Carolina. Isn't it that strange the same place I cried not to leave was the same place a few years later I did not want to go back to? I mean, I still had my childhood friends, but life for me here was good; I had made a good reputation for myself, our crew was respected, we were all into sports, the school was fun, and things were just great for me. Life was good. This led to somehow convincing my mom that I should stay with who was my best friend at the time, him and his family.

My best friend from Mississippi and his father ended up moving our senior year due to the split of his dad and stepmom. Convincing my mom of this was not that hard simply because I had stayed with him before for about thirty days when my parents had training for the military out in California. Our parents had a decent relationship, and we looked at each other like brothers. I was close with his family, and we did everything together, and his parents were huge supporters in supporting us in sports. They weren't missing anything. Besides, on the west coast, this was a thing that, again, I was not used to. Families would take their kids' friends in like it was nothing now. However, I was never kicked out of my house, which was also a trending topic. Out west, kids would be kicked out left and right like no joke and move into their friends' houses, and quite frankly, parents were okay with that. I had never experienced kids being kicked out of their homes before, and that it was a real thing, so it took some getting adjusted to.

My parents were off into their deployment when I started my senior year and would always have someone record my games and track meets and send them to them. I never even asked her how she was getting those recordings, but it was someone sitting in the stands. That's weird. Tonight, is the night that bond would break and never be the same again.

On the biggest night of my high school football career, it was our homecoming. The stands were packed, and the crowd at these types of schools was massive. It was insanely roaring as we entered the field. I was always the last one to come out. I don't know why it was just always my thing. The game ended up being a great one for me. We left our rivalry team with a goose egg, scoring zero points and being blown out by us a touchdown from myself and a few others. After the game, the supporters would run down and cheer us on while leaving the field, but the night got awkwardly fast. I noticed his parents weren't smiling, cheering on him, all excited like no mal. We were told to come straight home as if something had gone wrong because we would usually stop for food, talk about the game, get home, freshen up, and head back out the door to find something to get into on a Friday night. Tonight, was different. Entering the house, I was told to sit down and stay downstairs as he went upstairs, and then it began. His mom and dad, mainly his mother, were screaming at the top of their lungs. A situation had occurred with one of my Hispanic friends where he had a connection out in California where he knew a grower for marijuana and could get pounds of it at a discount rate. He planned to flood the school. Now, in the text messages, to my defense, I never said I was going to partake in anything. I just simply advised if he was going to do something like that, this would be the smarter way to do things and gave him a few tips on how he should go about doing things with calculations on what his profits would be. As stated before, I was a mastermind when it came to numbers, and it never took me long to figure out a few scenarios and then the possible best option for doing some ing. To pull something like this off, you would need a team you could trust. You weren't planning on getting your hands dirty yourself, were you? So those were the sorts of things I suggested via text message; I mean, it was just tipped to me. I mean, if you want to be a criminal, go right ahead but be a good criminal. Right? Be good at everything you do. If you weren't in it to reap the benefits, then why do something? His mom went through his phone and discovered our text messages, and word got back to my friend's parents. His mom swore that what I did was the worst thing on earth, his father was in the military, and I could get him kicked out that I was going to laundry drugs through their house and get them into some "deep shit" (she said it not me). I honestly did not see what the big deal was and thought they were blowing the situation way out of proportion; of course, I did not get the chance to explain myself, and honestly, once someone views me in a certain light, I don't care to try and explain myself. I took the wrap for the whole thing, and you think your son did not know what was going on when we did everything together, but okay, your story, I'll let you tell it. I remember being told aggressively to go to my room, don't turn on the tv, give me my phone, don't leave the house, and life had just turned into complete hell for me for about a month straight. She told my mom but forgot to mention how she was aggressively talking and cursing at me. Of course, my mom asked me what had happened, and I was going to sell drugs at school or period. I told her no and that I was telling him what to do because they weren't smart enough to figure it out. After that, my mom never repeated a word about it. In the next chapter, you'll soon enough find out the bond me and my mother had. I never had to hide anything from her, and she knew that we could talk about anything under the sun, and anything I did, my mom or stepdad would be the first to know. Like my fight with the kid at school where I got suspended for those few days, soon as I knew a kid was coming after school to fight me, I texted my parents that morning when I got to school so they would be aware. I just never had to hide anything, and my mom knew I was far from dumb I never got into serious trouble or made serious bad decisions other than the egging incident. I excelled in school and was just a good kid. I cared about clothes, shoes, and good grades. That's about it. We would always talk about the kids who had to hide things from their parents would be the ones who grew up reckless, and little did his mom know that's exactly what was happening; I mean, it never occurred to you that just maybe your son knew to and had a few ideas to make some money? Word got out at school by my Hispanic friend that I had messed up his whole operation and told on him to our parents, Yea; no one believed that or paid no attention. My reputation was just always that solid, and how I carried myself when that didn't work, he claimed he was going to fight me, but something tells me he came to his senses and decided not to do that either. Everyone knew I was too smart to get caught in a simple crossfire-like that. Wait, so Mack told your parents on you about your operation on something he wasn't even a part of but just telling you how you should do it if that were a route you were going to take, yet he's the only one facing the consequences, yes makes perfect sense (sarcastically speak ng). Strangely, being from the south, it was well respected in Washington. They thought highly of southerners, maybe because it wasn't something they were used to. Eventually, he just left it alone. Meanwhile, I was going through pure hell at my best friend's house; I did not want to eat, leave my room, or do anything. I never spoke out on the situation, but it ate me up inside to know this kind of picture was being painted towards me and they did not know any better based on how close we once were. My best friend tried to stay neutral, but of course, that did not work. Word has it, he said a few things, but I did not sweat it. We remained cool even after my parents came back from their nine-month deployment, but it was just never the same, and we eventually lost con act. My stepfather did not like what was going on at all, and quite frankly, I began to think these people were a little c lazy. Home and family I loved so much I began to feel resentment and hatred towards them; I even tried to move in with my track coach, who was also my football coach; however, due to legal reasons, it would just not be worth it, and my parents would be home in a couple of months anyway I just had to deal with it. For a month or so, I lost contact with my childhood friends. Just before this, my right-hand man snakehead had caught a charge of possession of a firearm and an assault charge, and that summer, was heading to DJ-J, a juvenile detention center, so everyone around me I would speak to was battling problems of their own. At the time, this was, in fact, that dark space again with a mixture of depression and heightened anxiety. My coach hated it as well. We would have talked before practice, and he knew my energy was just off. Leaving practice and then going home felt like judgment day every single day all over again, being singled out as I began to feel like I was just the worst, and this was all my f ult. Even having to apologize to try and release some of the tension in the house, apologizing for something I didn't even know what I was apologizing for because to me, I had still seen no wrong in what I had done and felt like the situation was taken way out of context, talk about a permanent scar that was one of them. These people were turning my world upside down. I mean, could you blame me for feeling the way I felt? I was not selling drugs, and who enjoys being blamed for something they know they're not doing? Doesn't it bother them? Well, eventually, my parents made it back home safe from deployment, and this was one of the happiest days of my life, and I was ready to get the hell out of there. My senior graduation rolled around. I remember telling my mom I still wanted to call and invite his parents to my graduation because although they may have seen me this way now, I did appreciate them wholeheartedly for what they had done, allowing me to stay with them for nine months while my parents were gone even though arrangements were made between our parents. I always had my own money based on losing my father at a young age. I'll never forget that call of my apologizing again for something I disagreed with and inviting them to my graduation, and what do you know, just as you've probably imagined. She started going on again about how you don't do people like that who allowed you into their home and how I was so wrong not to take life for granted. It would not get me anywhere in life. Everything to try hurt my teenage feelings all over again, just saying whatever came to her mind, I assumed and then declining the invite. At this point, I remember telling my parents about it! I was pissed, and if I had been a disrespectful child that day, I would have let her have it, but instead, I listened and minded my manners. So, to you, I would like to say thank you, you're a part of my story, and with things like this, I'm able to turn into positive energy and use it as motivation to keep going. Our families never spoke after that day, but my only question now is, looking from afar and seeing the man I've become, I can only wonder what you think of me now. Were you right about me?

"Someone is out there holding their breath waiting on you to fail, make sure they suffocate"

- Nita Ben.

CHAPTER

5

DEAR MAMA

*C*an *you hear me, mama? I need you now. Please pick up your phone. How could I ever forget? How would I ever forget?*

I remember standing in my third-grade classroom the morning of September 11, 2001, saying the Pledge of Allegiance like we would every morning. It was just another typical day for me. Then boom, breaking news nineteen terrorist hijackers had boarded four planes and marked one of the most vicious attacks of American history, claiming the lives of two thousand nine hundred ninety-six people and injuring far more. The hijackers had flown two planes into the world trade center known as the Twin Towers. A third plane, American Airlines flight 77, had struck the pentagon, and the fourth plane was United Airlines flight 93, whose target remains unknown. The theory is that it was meant for the U.S. Capitol or the White House. Still, courageous passengers avoided this and crashed outside Shanksville, Pennsylvania. How devastating. How heartbreaking. America at once was shattered into pieces. In return, this would declare The Global War on Terror that would mark the invasion into Afghanistan. American troops would begin dismantling Osama bin Laden and his Al-Qaeda organization, driving the Taliban away from power.

Tension escalated when the U.S. invaded Iraq in 2003, not accusing Saddam Hussein, dictator of Iraq, of having anything to do with 9/11 but allegations of being linked allies with Osama Bin Laden and his Al-Qaeda organization. This would change the U.S. government's views on terrorists forever and claim the lives of many prolific soldiers fighting for their country, lasting almost two decades after the decision to withdraw from Afghanistan came into effect in the early summer of 2021.

"Can you hear me, mama? I need you now. Please pick up your phone" were the cries of a little boy in 2002 when my mom became a part of that one percent to serve her country. Her first overseas duty station was in South Korea. So many nights as a child, my grandmother would rock me to sleep, or I would cry myself to sleep, whichever came first. I did not understand the military at all and what I knew was what I saw on TV; simply two enemies of their Army would meet in a vast open field and fight, killing each other until either side was destroyed first.

You could blame that on too many old western movies with my grandfather. As bad as I wanted my mother to pick up the phone and return home, she and her brother were off at war, and it's nothing I could do about it. As a child, my mother spent the majority of the time off doing Army things, but I never blamed her but rather the Army. Okay, if we're being honest here, I did blame her just a little for not being there. At least sometimes I wanted her when other kids had their mothers because that's only right. Oddly though, she would always call, and her presence was always felt. I thought she was off doing top-secret things that she could not discuss. I always knew my mother's identity and never had to question that part of the story. I would later change my viewpoint in understanding that having me at such a young age, seventeen, the sacrifices she made were all for me. Imagine how she must've felt having to leave her child behind, popping in and out of his life every time the Army calls—signing over the rights to her child while attending boot camp to her grandparents.

She cried like a baby when she had to sign those papers and begged my grandparents to promise that they would sign the legal parental rights back over to her after she completed boot camp. I never really asked further questions about that. I just assumed that when you're shipped out for boot camp, at least back then anyway, single mothers with kids would have to give legal guardianship to someone while they were away, which involved paperwork. I was entering the fifth grade when my mom finally got stationed at Fort Bragg, North Carolina, in Fayetteville. I attended Ashley elementary school, and for anyone traveling Owen Dr still today, which turns into All American Freeway to enter Fort Bragg, I stayed right in the Briarwood apartment complex, which is still open today.

The complex is a good size, but it was nothing special, and I imagine the rent was not that high compared to some of the other apartment complexes that Fayetteville offers. I remember my room; as a kid, it's nothing like having an excellent space for your favorite character, cartoon, football, or basketball team. Remember me mentioning my mom a very first overseas tour of her being stationed in South Korea? Well, guess what? My room was filled with Pittsburgh Steelers attire (my favorite football team). Everything was brought from Korea; you name it, I had it in a Steelers pattern. My lamp and comforter set included pillows, my clock, Pittsburgh Steelers posters, and even my name written in Korean on a scroll to hang on my door with collectible toy cars lined up going from one corner of my room to the other. If you have not noticed by now, everything I consumed or was around as a child is what I grew to love as an adult, especially cars; I had to have every hot-wheel vehicle back then. My mom supported my habits as a kid; of course, I was broke as a child, so it's up to our parents to keep our habits, right?

My mom had a friend who also lived in the apartment complex. Long story short, I hated this guy and remembered him being from Mississippi and having a funny accent. However, I must admit he had a nice SUV with the bass drowning out the words in the trunk so loud you could hardly hear yourself think when riding inside. After all, I still didn't like him, or what I'm trying to say is I did not like him for one simple reason and one simple reason only. He liked my mom; as a kid, anyone who wanted my mom did not sit right with me. I mean, come on, I'm a mama's boy. That's why we run off all our mother friends or make their life a living hell until they can't take it anymore and stop coming around; then our job is complete. It just grossed me out, and honestly, I don't think I even knew why I did not want my mom to be with anyone, and it had nothing to do with my dad. They were, in fact, cool with each other.

My dad was one of the lucky ones. He always handled his business and never ended up on child support. Maybe it was just thought of her being hurt by someone or thinking another man would try and come and be my dad or something. I don't know what I was thinking back then. All I knew was that I was overly protective of my mother and did not want any guys near her, every time she left the house as a kid, I would cry if I could not go with her. Oh man, did I have it wrong? It's pretty shameful as I write this, reminiscing, laughing, and shaking my head all that time. I remember hanging out with a couple of the homies in the complex when they had the idea to walk over to the gas station and buy a few snacks. Yes, even in the fifth grade, ten years old, I understood how to walk to the gas station. Right outside Briarwood apartments back then, you could take the sidewalk and walk right up to the gas station, a few paces that were not very far. There also was a Bojangles, a Pizza Hut, and McDonald's in that same lot, and today it has changed around a little to a more considerable lot for a McDonald's. Man, I could recall my first time eating Bojangles seasoned fries and thinking this was the best thing in the world, that is, until I discovered Cookout Cajun fries right down the street.

Fun fact: I love all fries, with Chic fil waffles fries being my favorite.

I went to the gas station with a couple of my homies who were brothers and had this bright idea that they would buy some snacks. Now, I had no money, but I still thought nothing of it; okay, let's go, and before you knew it, we were in the store then eventually walked out now; the funny thing is no one ever went to the counter and purchased anything quite sure of it. However, outside the store, my friends unload their pockets with candy and bubble gum. My first instinct was to take off. I don't know, maybe I panicked, but when you commit a crime, you take off running, right? You don't just stand there and wait for the police to do you? And might I add that the same year before moving to Fayetteville, North Carolina, I was with my dad's side of the family playing at Andrews elementary school playground one weekend when my cousin and I decided to try and open the doors to the school which sounded a silent alarm that brought the police to the school. My cousin got away, but I was left with our little cousin until Nana came to school and sorted everything out. So yea, I wasn't going to be the one getting caught and having run-ins with the police this time. So, I took off and didn't look back until I got home. "Not this time," I would think. I burst through the doors out of breath, telling my mother that, unfortunately, I don't remember their names, but let's say Tom and Jerry had stolen from the gas station, and I couldn't believe it. Come to think of it. I don't think my mom paid much attention. She might've asked what happened and where they were now, so I eventually calmed down and brought my heartbeat back down to a steady pace. Wooah! that could've been a close one, I thought; nothing happens, and in a matter of minutes, I would notice them from our balcony playing outside like nothing ever happened. I went back outside to join in as they asked man, your fast. Where did you take off to? I might've stared away from the question responding with something like I almost forgot I had to get home to do something for my mom. It was going to be you guys. I had just stolen, and I was scared the cops would be on my tail, and I did not want any parts of it. Yes, I was only ten, but by this time in my life, I understood who cops were and probably had already seen too much to be ten years old; at this time in my world, coming from where I'm from, cops were only in the hood for one reason, and that's to arrest someone you didn't wait around to find out either. It was always the thought of getting in trouble that would make me panic or heart beat out of my chest, sort of like that being drunk or high feeling, things I can't control I never liked. This brings me to the point of me getting in trouble. This particular day after school, outside playing, maybe I had; had a long day and wasn't in the mood. Those same guys, for the sake of this book, Tom and Jerry, were all outside playing with some more people and their little sister when all of a sudden, it looked like she was trying to run me over with the bike. My first reaction was what? Well, of course, to dodge her and push her off the bike; remember that balcony I mentioned? Well, we lived on the second floor, and my mother saw everything storming out the door and calling me upstairs. She had a nice black belt waiting on me and beat me with a couple of swings to my behind with it. Now, I cried, but I think I was more in disbelief. My mom was yelling and just gave me a whooping. For one, my mom never raised her voice. Even still today, she's not going to yell. Just say whatever it is and be done with it, let alone get mad. I can probably count how many times I've seen my mom upset. I did not understand why I got beaten. She was trying to run me over with the bike, but she later explained that she was still a girl and it wasn't nice to push her off the bike like that, falling to the ground, not to put your hand on girls. I swear it seems like I was always taught a lesson growing up. That was the last day my mom ever beat me; see, I told you she just was not the type to be upset, which brings me to mind when you read this; how come you got upset that one day? Maybe it was work or her friend who had her uptight, and she just wanted to let off some steam on me. That's it. Not quite a full year in Fayetteville, only one school term, I was being hauled back off to Oatland, South Carolina, where I'm from. Don't worry. It's not on the map, so don't try to look it up. Duty had called, and my mom was leaving yet again, this time headed to Iraq to serve her country doing twelve months which then turned into being extended to fifteen months. Did the Army not think these deployment lengths were excessive for soldiers to be away from their families? I mean, twelve and fifteen months off into a warzone in the desert in this time of environment and living conditions was ridiculous, I thought actually, and so did someone else who mattered with a voice because it was later in return reduced to nine-month deployments which still seems a bit much when the Air Force only does six months at a time. I remember returning to South Carolina and trying to keep in contact with my two best friends, Mark and Nicholas. At the time when meeting this was funny.

Mark and Markus are two best friends. Our cell phone contact eventually faded; yes, I had always had a cell phone since the fifth grade. My mom thought it was wise, and it was how my dad and I talked daily. My mom thought it was wise because, believe it or not, sometimes I would have to get myself up for school and walk to the bus stop, and I don't blame my mother at all. It's not easy being a single mother and trying to raise a son. As mentioned, duty sometimes would call, and she would have to be at the worktop in the morning and could not see me off to school. Now, this was, in fact, maybe dangerous, but she was also good friends with a family downstairs in those apartments that would also check on me when work had to be a priority; anytime I would oversleep, I would call her and let her know if she could, she would come off base and take me to school if not I just sat home. However, we were on a pretty good routine. I knew how to get up and get ready for school, put on my clothes, and do my hygiene; I knew what to do in case of emergencies, so honestly, anything going wrong I never thought about, and besides, even at the age of ten certain things I just was not a stranger too. I did miss those Fayetteville days, though. Back then, I was into going to the skating rink and skating with rollerblades; the only way I know how to skate still today is with rollerblades. Which makes me wonder if I still got it. I was good at it. I also enjoyed soccer back then, and I don't know if I just enjoyed running or what because it seems like that's all we did, just running all over the place chasing a soccer ball, but I enjoyed it. I do not miss the times my mother deployed; I remember it being a sad day full of tears. No matter how often she left or how long we knew beforehand, she would squeeze the life out of me with a bear hug as we were both just standing there crying. Again, as a mother, I knew it was breaking her inside every time she had to leave her only son at the time behind, but I also think she understood the sacrifice was to be able to provide for me a better living. Working at Walmart and nice restaurants wasn't just going to cut it for her anymore, and even though I was from where I was from, I still was never the child that went without. Some people blow up and begin fabricating their stories to make them sound better, but not me. Rather it came from my mother, aunt, and uncles. I was never really the child to go without or didn't have food on the table with clothes on my back. The saying is very much so true. I was raised in a village, and during the days in my little country area, most kids took a community. This deployment lasted my sixth-grade year before she would return and get the station at Fort Drum, New York, and then to Fort Lewis, Washington, in the middle of my tenth-grade year when I finally would leave South Carolina again, moving twice in one year New York than Washington. By this time came along she had married my stepdad. I remember finding out she was conversing with him over the phone. Remember, I was always super protective over my mother and felt like no man was good enough for her, so no one knew what my reaction would be. Thinking back on it, that's funny now. So, our conversation went a little like this, my first question, randomly speaking, was, "do you drink" surprisingly, he said no, hmmm, okay, I thought, what kind of guy doesn't drink? Well, if we're being honest, the older I got, quite a few people drink, but many people also don't drink. Okay, let me try this, "do you smoke" he said no, "do you put your hands on women" yea, that's right, a fifteen-year-old boy was asking these kinds of questions, and I couldn't seem to catch him up in anything, so I could yell out mom "see he's not the one for you!" So, I gave the if she likes it, I love it type of response, and that was that. Now, you might be wondering, wow, Mack, you didn't even try and get to know the guy at all or ask where he was from, no, nothing. Well, my grandmother had already told me he was from Mobile, Alabama, and getting to know him, I did not care about it at the time if we were being honest. Those were the questions that were important to me, and I needed him to know that, and my stepdad was huge and on/off in the gym. He, for sure, was no pushover at about six-three two hundred forty pounds. I stood back then, maybe five four five-five one hundred twenty-seven pounds, but that didn't matter to me. I was told at twelve years old when my father closed his eyes I had to stand up and be a man now, so that's what I was doing. The truth is, maybe I'm just now getting over the fear of someone putting their hands on my mother and me killing them, and now I'm spending the rest of my life in prison. Back then, it was just something I stood on wholeheartedly. You hurt my mother. You touch her. I'm killing you end of discussion. Man, that's extreme. Yes, it was, but I think people have grown to know that I've always tried to be a man of my word so thank God for growth, right? You know what? I remember when my mom had a small knot right over her eye. I can not remember if it was a bite from an insect or her downloading some supplies from an upper armored LMTV from work in the military and something catching her in the head. Long story short, I was pissed! I took it upon myself not even asking to assume she had got into an altercation with someone, and now it was time to see where this person was, right?

She sat me down and explained what had happened, as it slowly felt like I could breathe again. Okay, wooaaahhh, that was a close one. However, my stepdad would later become someone I once looked up to, or maybe it was the materialistic things he had. He loved cars, jewelry, Call of Duty, and what seemed to make my mom happy. They were always out doing something, traveling, seeing the world, something, and in Washington, we had three nice homes. Yup, you read that right. Even after all this moving back and forth from state to state due to them deploying in Washington and having different training, we also moved to three different houses in the three years we lived there. Two in the same neighborhood and one in a neighborhood not even 10 minutes away. Our house was always the hangout spot for the kids. Everyone thought my parents were cool. I cannot make this up; I mean, I did too. My stepdad loved cracking jokes and being funny. My mom has always been more shy, quiet to herself never says too much, but she can talk your ear off once she opens up. Kids could be themselves at my house, all while fighting over my mother's famous red velvet cake, jambalaya rice, fried chicken wingettes, and drumettes with some macaroni and cheese on the side. Uhm, Uhm, good, delicious, everyone loved that meal. Life was not bad in Washington. As stated, I had plenty of cultural backgrounds as friends, my mind was expanding, and I was getting to see something different. My mother and I were tighter than superglue. Would you believe these women tried to race me on foot once? Yea, I know what you're thinking but wasn't her son the fastest kid in the school yea I know, right? That's exactly what I said! She was trying me that day, but that's just the kind of relationship we had. Some would say your parents can't be best friends with their kids. I would beg to differ with my mother, and I did it for years, and I'd like to think I turned out just fine, even with some of the sacrifices she made, missing some of my track meets, me running in the championships, my football games, and even my prom. Duty called, and she was doing what she had to do to protect her son's country and provide for him. So, I never tried to make her feel bad about anything or even wanted her to. No matter how nice it would've been to have her there, I understood what was happening and what was at stake. Even today, our bond remains close-knit, but I try to let my little brother take up most of her attention and time nowadays. That's right, about nineteen years later, just when I thought I would be the only child forever and my mom was down, I guess she and my stepdad decided to have a child, Omari, my little brother. Maybe the Honolulu, Hawaii weather, once they left Washington and got station there, ran the breeze of a baby fever right across their front door.

My little brother being born did not give me a sense of jealousy but rather the kind of man I'm about nineteen years older than my little brother. However, I was still proud to be a big brother and recalled asking my mom, so nineteen years later, huh, you waited this long? But I guess, as the good book says, timing is everything, or maybe she just got bored after I left the nest. Who knows. I never made it to Hawaii, going for about three years without seeing my mother or even meeting my little brother in person, not at least until they made it to Fort Belvoir in Virginia.

I got the chance to see my mom in mommy mode, which was weird seeing her tend to another child beside me, if we're being honest. So, these are the things you did when I was a toddler and a baby. I remember my little brother having a lot of energy and running around everywhere, and either my stepdad or mom chasing him around the house.

Here's where I insert my next permanent scar putting a shift in the story, trying to make someone who may read this one day go, "Not again. He's already been through enough." So, the boom, here we go. It's time for my stepdad and mom to move again after a few years of being stationed in Virginia for what's known as a PCS move, a permanent change of station. Their next stop was South Korea, and unfortunately, my stepdad never made it to Korea. The news was coming out that was all new to me and quite surprising. It was rather unbelievable. He treated my mother like a queen worshiping the ground she walked on. None of this can't be true. The man I grew to love and look up to left me devastated and disappointed.

Fun Fact: I have never seen or heard them argue. I would always think my stepdad and mom were like Michelle and Obama. Okay, that's a stretch. Let's try Russell Wilson and Ciara; let's go with that. We did live in Washington, and he did play for Seattle Seahawks. In so many words, their relationship seemed perfect to me, and growing up through high school, if I was going to marry anyone, this is what I wanted it to be like. Instead, I got something different and slowly began to resent and hate my stepdad.

Knowing me, you would know that I never try and use the word hate. To me, it's just a strong word and to hate something is highly disgusting. Hate is a very passionate, strong word when describing something you dislike. So, yes, I started to hate my stepdad, and we had a great relationship. It's just the way our household was. I mean, could you blame me for hating a man that made my mother shed tears that sent her through depression with an escalation of anxiety for someone she may have thought she would spend the rest of her life with? Keep in mind my mother and I could always talk about anything, so these may be uncomfortable conversations about a separation or a divorce, how she felt and tried to hold her marriage together long enough, and what she was going through I knew about, and I felt. It affected me tremendously and took a toll on my mental my mom was in pain, and I felt like it was nothing I could do to instantly wipe those tears and pain of suffering away after a bad breakup of well over a decade of being together. I had to do something; what could I do? So, without anyone's knowledge, I found my stepdad on Facebook messenger after his name change and wrote him one of the longest, most scrutinizing messages in history. It started with calling him every name in the book you could think of, expressing what I would do to him if I ever ran into him, even threatening him to drop his address location if he was a man and we would see who the bigger man was. The paragraphs of nastiness I was sending my stepdad came from anger and hurt from just letting me down and my love for my mother. You just weren't supposed to be one of the ones who became a part of that divorce statistic and failed me, putting a stereotype on yet another marriage, let alone another black marriage that fails. The truth is, I was hurt, and it changed my life.

The family I was used to was no more. Do I wish I could take it back? Not it's how I felt at the time. Was I wrong? I made it my business by taking everything personally to the extreme. To someone who made read this one day, if you haven't already noticed, I'm not good at dealing with failing; I overreact and think it's the end of the world. I just do not like failing at something, a test grade, anything, or even being associated with things or people that fall, and that's exactly what I felt like my stepdad had done, and it was not sitting right with me at all. Today I'm brave enough to say to my stepdad once, wherever you may be as I type this, I forgive you; I'm afraid I have to disagree with how you went about things, but I forgive you and now understand that life happens. You or I cannot take back the many memories we shared, and for that, I'll hold on to them and remember you as the great man I once knew you to be. I'll always have much love and respect for you for the good things you did do, and I understand that lessons learned all come as being a part of life. I cannot enjoy the fruits of my labor without letting that dark hole of what you and my mother went through continue to weigh in on me, but instead, I find it in my heart to forgive. Wherever you are and whatever you may be doing, I wish you the best, Gucci. (The nickname I gave him a long time ago). Isn't it funny how times change? Here we go thanking God for growth again.

"You always were a black queen, mama; I finally understand. For a woman, it isn't easy trying to raise a man. You always were committed.

*There's no way I can pay you back, but I plan to show you that
I understand: you are appreciated"*

- Tupac.

CHAPTER

6

ME VS ME

October 21, 2013, fall is setting in, and the cool chill breeze is beginning to jump-start your morning to wake you fully. The time of year when you walk outside and start your car to warm up before you get inside. Within the blink of an eye, I was on a one-way trip riding on Fort Jackson, South Carolina, on a bus with my head face down into a green duffle bag per our Drill Sergeant as he was screaming different things obnoxiously at the top of his lungs. I said I would never join the Army because I blamed the military for some of the times my mother missed, but shit happens. I mean, we've all heard the saying never say, never, right?

I'll never forget that day with a clean shaved head, squeezing my eyes so tightly closed face down into my green duffle bag, afraid that if I looked up to our Drill Sergeant, all hell would break loose. Instantly, I would think, "Lord, what did I sign up for?"

Arriving at our unit, whose motto was "Always Forward," about four buses of soon-to-be soldiers would jump off as my battle buddies. I scrambled for our respective drill pads and what platoon we would be in. It must've been about fifty Drill Sergeants that day, male and female, with Hercules syndrome pumping through their veins, causing an uproar and chaos everywhere, knocking people's bags over, and yelling at them to run faster. Yet, I'm carrying about a fifty-pound duffle bag with all my gear inside. Before going through pure hell, let's not mention calling your family one last time. Who would've ever thought a two-minute phone call would end so fast?

We were off to the races, and please, for the love of me, could you guys stop yelling and knife-hand-pointing at everyone? To someone who may read this one day, I know that it will be a few of you who will read this and instantly know what I'm talking about, reminiscing about the nervous shocks that ran through your body on the first day of boot camp and the big ole fat question mark that would begin to surface your membrane about what the hell you had just got yourself into. This story inside of a story still makes me laugh today.

So boom, everyone was in standard formation, and one kid was balling his eyes out in tears. He's surrounded by Drill Sergeants so close to him that their Drill Sergeant hat is maybe just centimeters from butting the guy in the forehead, you could see spit buds flying this guy's mouth, and they were giving him the business as he's just balling his eyes out in tears. One drill sergeant yells, "YOU WANT TO QUIT? YOU WANT TO GO HOME?!"

The guy is crying and sighs back slightly, "Yes."

Here goes the drill sergeant, "WHAT WOULD YOU SAY TO YOUR SON IF HE WANTED TO QUIT AT SOMETHING?" The poor guy screams with tears in his eyes, "I WOULD TELL HIM TO QUIT, DRILL SERGEANT."

Lord, why in the hell did he do that? Adding more fuel to the fire, this lasted another fifteen minutes of them drilling this guy, and still, to this day, I have no idea how they knew he had a son. So that passed, and at 4 AM sharp the next morning, we were standing tall, chanting the soldier's creed loudly, getting ready to take our first physical fitness test. I knew this would be where I would make my mark. In 2013, the educational background was important in the military but not as popularized as today. Back then, your First Sergeant loved a good soldier who was good at PT (physical fitness). I was eighteen at the time, so max points of a hundred in each category would be seventy-one push-ups, seventy-five sit-ups, and a two-mile run of thirteen minutes or less. The max for Physical fitness was three hundred points, and exceeding any of these points according to the age bracket of your standard would put you on the extended scale. Of course, I showed up with me and a few other guys, not many but a couple of others, even overlapping people. This would set the tone of who the drill sergeants, for the most part, would take it easy on because, in a sense, they had biased opinions towards soldiers that excel in PT. Not only that, but I could march (drill & ceremony), and was no slow leak to tests and book smarts. This made basic training sort of a cakewalk for me but just eventually got tired of being isolated from what felt like the world; my head was constantly shaved bald, and maybe three phone calls my entire training for a couple of minutes, and although things came easy to me I was just over it and ready to get back to being myself. However, just like anything else, it's exactly what you make of it, and most people would take the drill sergeant antics personally, not understanding that it's just their there profession, it's just business, and that's why they're who they're. I mean, you think the average male walking around would be sitting in the defect (cafeteria) one day eating his chow (food) as fast as Major Payne and then suddenly standing up and starting going ham at a soldier because he took his eyeballs off his plate to raise his head and look up. Well, yea, that was my Drill Sergeant. He saw this and went nuts, flipping over chairs and shouting at the top of his lungs. Yup, it was time for me to go and get out of there. This guy was insane, and it's not like I would eat most of my food anyway. I struggled with only having 2-3 minutes to eat from when you sat down, or did you expect me not to chew my food properly and choke? I eventually got with the program as the weeks went on. However, it was still a struggle for me most times, I would grab French Toast for breakfast, and that's how I fell in love with French Toast with a side of syrup at basic training. They were always so deliciously soft and warm, during lunch I mainly would use peanut butter packets to fill me and by the time dinner came, I was so tired I didn't want to eat much anyway but get back to the dorm shower and be standing tall at 4 AM all over again day after day PT after PT as we marked the days off the calendar in our dorm. Leaving in October for basic training, I would, of course, miss Thanksgiving and then I began to understand the meme post about praying for soldiers serving our country and anyway from loved ones and family. That day we got to eat a little longer with a nice dinner, but it was still not the same. Still, of course, we were all hanging in together, wondering what the outside world was done without access to a tv or phone. At night people would either be fast to sleep or turn on their red flashlight to write a letter and get them sent out in the morning before the drill sergeant stormed in bright and early, turning over wall lockers and banging on things to wake us. For the record, after the first day, I understood it didn't take long to adapt and understand that I was here strictly on business; however, little did I know other plans were right around the corner for me. It's now December, a few days before we get to go home on holiday block leave and then come back, and that would leave us about two weeks away from graduation. We had just completed the popular Knick at night that everyone who's been through the Army basic training will never forget, your low crawling what seems to be about two football fields, while grenades are going off, tracer rounds are going off and flying overhead and what do you know it for me it starts raining and pitch black at night. It seems like this field is never-ending. I'm sure that's probably one of everyone's most talked about memorable exercises during basic training, that or your first time experiencing the gas chamber. I wasn't sure if I was training to become a soldier or if these people were trying to kill me at that point. The next day was a long day at the weapons range that I did not mind because I enjoyed shooting, especially when we got to drive and shoot at night with the NVGs on Night Vision Googles. So, then boom we were back from the weapons range that day and a calm walk-in from my three drill sergeants that First Sergeant needed to see me in his office. Now, of course, I have no idea what this could be for, and all I could think about was, "Oh, wow, you guys aren't yelling per usual that's different," and not to mention how did you guys' yell so much anyway without getting hoarse hmmm must be the training. We enter the First Sergeant's office. I go to parade rest as he quickly calls me to at ease and tells me to have a seat as my drill sergeants are standing off to the left rear and right of me. He goes into the casual conversation, asking me how basic training was going for me, how I was doing, and so on. Well, everything is going well. First Sergeant, thanks for asking. He opens a folder and begins reading a well-formatted document. As he was reading, it did not take me long to figure out that he was talking about my great-grandmother. She had taken her last breath just a few days before I would return home. Honestly, I can only remember going off into a blank stare with tears rolling down my face, and I was no longer even paying attention to what the red cross message had said, so that's not a question I could answer. The last words I remember were Bernice Cuttino, my great-grandmother. He closed by sending his condolences, was there anything they could do? Did I need anytime to see a chaplain? Did I need to speak to anyone or even call my family? I might've spoken with my grandmother for a couple of minutes, but the conversation did not last long. With everyone in the room trying to brace me and sympathy. I remember quoting these words "with all due respect. I'm used to it."

This surprised everyone because they did not understand what I was saying and looked shocked. I explained that I was just numb to death as a tear would roll down my eyes here and there. My first sergeant still seemed a bit confused, so I tried to the best of my ability to explain to everyone in the room what I meant by being numb to death. Top, it's just something I'm used to; I've lost my great-grandfather, my father, my grandfather, my uncle is in prison, and not to mention the countless others who have died from my hood. Why would anything else change for me now? They were all adamant about trying to change my view on life and death, and why it's not something you should grow used to but at this point, it just wasn't something I was ready to hear at that point in my life. I also felt like from the ages of 11-18 as a teen. They probably had not experienced anything like that so early on in life, if they had at all, even still as adults. So, in a sense, people I felt couldn't relate immediately boxed out, which now I know was not the right answer. I remember the feeling of being at my great-grandmother's funeral, everyone around me was devastated; my heart shattered into pieces as the church filled the melody with many cries. Truthfully, I was there, but I wasn't. The anger and hate that began to develop inside me would not allow me to put myself in a position to be hurt again; the pain I balled up and buried deep. I shed a few tears, but I was tired of it, and just like before, I had lost faith and was living to live.

I remember questions rapidly firing into my head like I try so hard to steer right when mass murders, child molesters, people who commit these outrageous crimes, and nothing bad happens to them what, a prison sentence that they still get to one day come home from and live. How's that any fair to me? Why should I do right? It gets me nothing but an added Permanent Scar every time I'm sick and tired of feeling broken! & with that, that's the mentality I began to develop, running from the thought of being hurt, and boy, it took a toll on my life in so many different ways. I was not going to allow myself to be put in a situation where I'd be hurt again; I had to mute those emotions and go numb, this was just how the tragedies of my life had taken place, and it was what it was. Did I sign up for this? Of course not, but these are the cards that were dealt, and I had to play my hand according to what I thought was best. Have you ever tried running away from the feeling of being hurt? If you have, you know it's no easy task, so it's wise never to look back, or you may find yourself tripping up over your foot. Getting in your way, as humans, we often do that; get in our head and at this point in my life, due to so many untimely demises of unfortunate events, little did I know I was contributing to destroying myself mentally. I was, in fact, in my head and in my way, tripping up over my footsteps. Now, let's get back to basic training two weeks before all our hard work and field exercises would pay off. We would graduate then, headed to Advanced Individual Training (AIT) for our respective Military Occupational Specialties (MOS). I would never forgive myself if I didn't share with someone who may read this one day, the famous fight night in the open thirty-to-forty-man dorm we were housed in bunk beds. Now, I'm a light sleeper and always have been. Earlier that day drill sergeant was on our case about a kid who had lost two hundred bulks even after smoking us and making us run up and down the stairs with sandbags dumping it on our dorm floor and spreading it around; we would clean it up, then he would make us go downstairs grab more sandbags repeating the process all over again. Finally, my battle and I had enough, and I decided to tell the drill sergeant it was me who took the money out of the guy wall-locker. Come to think of it, why did he have that kind of cash on him in basic training? I mean, it's not like you could buy much of anything anyway; however, that did not matter. Someone had stolen it, and that wasn't right. So, this time when we run back up to our floor with the sandbags, I'm going to tell drill sergeant I took the money, he tried to talk me out of it, but I went along with it anyway. Long story short, I just remembered him telling me to shut the hell up and a few words along with that. It was obvious that he knew I couldn't have possibly been a candidate for stealing the money. Welp, guys, I tried, and the smoking session continues for someone who may read this one day but's not familiar with the Army terminology. To be smoked means what some of you might have seen on television. For example, drop and give me fifty pushups, run over there then run back, do a hundred jump and jacks, hold a sandbag over your head without bending your arms; a smoke session could consist of all sorts of things which later throughout my career became a thin line between a smoke session and hazing a soldier. I will say this no one confessed to the drill sergeant, but by later that night, the word was out because what's the quickest way for news to travel? Word of mouth. It was said that a black guy had taken the money, and he was who everyone was pointing the finger at, and lord and behold, the guy he took the money from was white.

Well, well, well, later that night, when everyone was sound asleep, I woke up to five guys running through the bay and there hollering what sounded like Native American Indian noises with shirts wrapped around their heads and what I later found out was locks in a sock in there hand running to the guy who was accused of stealing the money and waking him up out of his sleep with a beating coming from every angle. He kicked, screamed, wiggled, and tried everything he could to get out of those guys' reach, but it was pitch black dark he wasn't getting away that easily with one guy holding a red flashlight on him to keep him in their line of sight they were on him like white on rice. They quickly retreated to their bunks when they thought he had had enough. Now I must say the guy took his beating like a grown-up, and although it was never proven, maybe he did steal the money because it was something they knew that the rest of us didn't. The next day the drill sergeant could not help but notice, and matters worsened. He was moved from our bay, and they tried everything they could to get everyone to crack, but two weeks out from graduation, no one wanted no part of that and mainly felt like, well, he cost it on himself and shouldn't have taken the money.

I got along with everyone, so I knew who the leader was, the mastermind behind the idea, and everything. See, going to a school with various background cultures, it was never hard for me to fit in where I needed to. The guy graduated but honestly, I don't remember seeing him much, if any, after that night except the morning, and let me tell you about the knot under his eye and on his forehead that looked like a mini baseball. It was huge, and I'm not even sure if someone held up three fingers, he would know how many fingers they were holding up, man what a time to be in basic training.

AIT was pretty much the same. Nothing complicated, and my instructor is someone I can give credit to that taught me the 360-wave game. There you have it. That's who fathered me in the hair game. Of course, he would instruct and teach us the study material, but during breaks, he would always have a brush and brush his hair. He did not play about the waves in his head. As you probably guessed, I had to know what those were. I thought they were just ripples, and with a drop of water, they would eventually appear. So, every day after class, he began giving me what I like to call "Free Game," his hair regiment routine, the products he used, his favorite brush from soft to medium to hard, at what stage to use what meeting, and even how low to get it cut. He explained that developing 360-waves was no easy task, and it took hard work and dedication. I thought, man, it's just hair, but boy was I wrong. Just like him, I began to take it seriously, and before you knew it, those ripples were starting to appear, and that was my motivation. I kept a brush any little second I had I was brushing. That's what AIT consisted of for me just getting through the days and passing up time. I did not study much for the test, but for the most part, I asked a lot of questions in class and always participated, which in return would help me to learn the study material faster. To pass the time, I also got talked into being a part of the Drill and Ceremony team.

Our routine was fire, and I could march, but the kid could twirl his weapon around his finger, throw it up behind his back high into the air, coming down with it like the ROTC kids off Major Payne. That won it for us. I also remember early mornings before getting ready for class. I would add 15 minutes to pull that black satin durag off and brush my hair. It took my whole AIT about three months, and by the time I got to my first duty station, my hair was trained and spinning so hard you might get seasick if you stared too long. My first duty station was Fort Hood, Texas, the same as my father. What a coincidence, right? This whole thing may be meant to be. Three of my big cousins were already stationed in Texas, two being brothers, so was this like the family being relocated to Texas or something? It's not every day that family members are constantly getting stationed at the same duty station. Still, if you know Fort Hood, it's a huge one of the most significant installations in the world, and a ton of people experience Fort Hood at least once throughout their military career. My first day on base, and I will be staying in reception for about ten days to process the floor and get everything scared away paperwork-wise before being shipped to your unit. This is the first step for every PCS move reception in processing through the clinic, household goods, dental, and so on. My first day was over, and I called my cousin to see his whereabouts, to let him know I had made it to Fort Hood safe and sound. His younger brother had just deployed a couple of weeks beforehand to Afghanistan. This day was the first start of my alcoholic journey.

Now I know I said I did not drink or smoke, but again shit happens. What can I say? Besides, the book is titled Permanent Scars, so I must share the good, the bad, and the ugly. My cousin picked me up and off to his barracks. Everyone was sitting around drinking and playing cards, spades, to be exact. Peer pressure is something else, but of course, I wasn't going to punk out, so guess what? Let's drink, "Ayyeeee pour me up cuz!" The rest was history, and I still don't remember much but waking up to a cold floor, drooling with a headache to die for. Luckily it was going into the weekend Saturday morning, and guess what my cousin and his friends wanted to do that day? Please wake up, go to the shoppette on the base, where it's tax-free and buy more bottles. WAIT! You all want to do what?! I'm still trying to recover from last night, and I'm not even sure where I'm at! I remember my cousin and his friends bursting into laughter, "Yea, cuz we bout to get fucked up again, this isn't nothing new we do this every day." Lord, what have I gotten myself into? You got to be kidding me, right? Again, I wasn't going to punk out. It was April, I was eighteen, and my birthday was next month on the eighteenth, I'm a man now, and just like going numb to death, I had to make the decisions I thought were best for me. Well, that was not the best decision I could've made and would not be my last. I quickly discovered that during this time, my cousin and his friends loved Svedka Vodka, a very popularized cheap vodka where the big 1.75-liter bottle only cost $17.99 with a few bucks to save out of that twenty-dollar bill. Now, why was this their go-to drink? It could get many people drunk for less because it tasted horrible. Their second go-to drink was Seagram's Extra Dry Gin, the 750-milliliter bottle for $14.99. Yea, that was the starter pack. It didn't take too many sips to start feeling good; before you knew it, you were somewhere wasted. Meanwhile, I eventually made it to my unit, and it was time to show up and show out again another Physical Fitness test. This would be a breeze. Why? Because at this point, it's all the first sergeants cared about for setting the bar pretty much was PT. I was hitting the vast scale on eighty pushups and eighty-five sit-ups and just getting up to walk away and stretch to prepare for the last part of the test, the two-mile run. I knew I had the first sergeant, the commander, and the platoon sergeant's attention; who's this new private? This is how I would set the tone at every unit I went to excel in PT, and the rest was up to me to shine bright like a diamond. On this PT test day, others were taking their PT test, of course, and it was talked about this specialist in a different platoon from what I would be in being the fastest person in the company out of

California. I knew I had a point to prove, and off to the races we went. I remember those runs I hated going on with my father when I could not stop running. Little did I know he was training me for moments like this. So, I kept my composure, staying within the distance of the fast guy from California, he was fast, but I knew once we got to the mile mark. At the turnaround point, he would have to show me what kind of heart he had because I always believed you would have to be pretty much willing to come near death to outwork me, and if you could pull that off, well, you, my friend, deserved it. In through your mouth and out breathe son breathe. I could hear my pops giving me those coaching lessons repeatedly, in and out, in and out. We arrived at the turnaround point; it was game on as I heard the Sergeant at the mile marker turnaround point say over his phone to those waiting on us to return their coming back. Granted, for the many others who were taking the test, this was all about me and you, friend, and my strategy was always to stay within striking distance of the first mile, conserving my energy while the guy out front was pumping hard trying to outrun me. It was time to turn it on, and I did. I remember getting beside him, and he tried as much as possible, but he couldn't take it. His heart wasn't as big, and he was not ready to come near death to outwork me. I began to step off, and as we were approaching, there was chanting, and now I was in a full-blown sprint, arms pumping hard as ever, breathing in and out as my father taught me, and I was all In crossing the finish line first sergeant yells in excitement 12.05! Yup that'll do it. My platoon sergeant goes ballistic in excitement. It was always a friendly competition in the unit, and we were now on top with bragging rights. The other guy still maxed out his PT test, but he did not outscore me on the extended scale, and you could tell by the expression on his face that he was a little disappointed in himself and that there was a new sheriff in town. However, it did not take long before we became friends, and that's how it went for me in my first unit. Who was Private Cuttino; where's he from? What's his MOS? All sorts of questions are as such. I began to develop my swag in uniform. I would take them to the cleaners to get pressed and keep my boots nice and neat with no dirt stands because, to me, appearance meant everything. Every Friday for lunch, I was at my barber getting a fresh cut who would eventually become a good friend of mine. Even while working, I had to look good while doing it. Why? Because believe it or not, everyone is judged based on the smallest things and appearance, along with cleanest is one of them. No holes or steins in the uniform, and everything dresses right to dress as it should be.

Now, everything was not so sweet for me. Yes, I struggled with being in a professional environment. My speech and, my language, my vocabulary see, I was from South Carolina where we were raised with a Geechee accent. I struggled because it worked when I was amongst my family and friends, but I was now out and into the real world, a professional environment, and the world Nigga was not allowed. Yes, embarrassing enough, I have been corrected a few times about the use of that word so strongly and frequently being in my vocabulary. I was no longer back in the hood, and for a while, when talking. People would stare at work. They had no idea what I was saying and always asked huh, what? Say that again. This grew frustrating and made me feel ashamed to be where I was from; I did not understand; how did you not know what I was saying?! I'm saying it clear as day, well to me, it sounded fine, but to them, I was not pronouncing my words properly or fully, I was talking way too fast, and it was like we had invented our language and vocabulary. Yup, that was it. My language and culture were different. My platoon sergeant took me under his wing, the conversations grew longer, and the bond grew stronger. I mean, this cat was smooth straight out of North Carolina, and he loved cars but get this, everything he did, he was good at it and looked good while doing it.

His uniforms were always clean, and he led by the example of what a well-solid platoon should look like. This brother had a soul; he could call cadence with soul, like singing in the church choir. He had a few cars, but his Cadillac and GMC Sierra were my favorites, and I'll never forget the day he told me, "Yea, man, I put wheels on everything."

He sat me down daily until I understood how things go in the military and how to succeed. The first thing first, he would say was, "Be good at your job. Be the best and give them nothing to talk about. Always go above and beyond."

He metaphorically explained that compared to a game, taking nothing for granted, deployments can get real and take full advantage of all benefits, especially education. Look, here's your promotion points worksheet, and here's how you read it and what category gives me what points to get promoted. He drilled in me how to always stay one step ahead, and many of his thought processes would resemble one of my favorite reads to date, the 48 Laws of Power.

Before you knew it, I was looking at him in the eyes of a father figure; any game he could give, he was giving it. In the miss of him getting me to enroll in an online college, teaching me how to work smarter, not harder, excelling at my job, and more, I still had one huge problem after work hours that were waiting on me heavily. By this point, my alcoholic beverage intake was increasing, and I was drinking like a fish. On countless occasions, he would save me for not showing up to morning formations, telling me to go to the barracks room and get myself ready for work. He could always smell the liquor screaming from my pores and would be quick to protect me from the eyes of others because of how they saw me in the perfect light, but little did they know outside of work, I had developed a serious drinking problem which seemed to be no big deal to me at the time. I mean, it wasn't good. I even had an incident where I ran from the military police on base in my white Impala SS.

They eventually came to my room, and I continuously denied knowing what they were talking about. They gave me a stern talking to, that even though I would not admit it, the trouble I could have gotten into underage drinking, let alone taking military police on many high-speed chases on base. This was not the end of my rodeo, as my platoon sergeant always protected me when calling for his help and how I should go about finessing things. It seemed like no matter how hard I was trying to put myself in trouble, something or someone always seemed to be watching over me and giving me a chance after chance. My homies out here were all I had.

I'm miles away from home, my mother is stationed in Hawaii, and we were young, wild, and turned up. I guess this made me feel that I still had a connection to that small country area I was from the streets of route 4, South Carolina and that I wasn't turning my back on anyone or leaving my childhood friends behind. Then soon enough, it would hit me one night of serving 24-hour staff duty at work. One of my childhood friends from our old crew, Swish We Balling, would make a split-second decision that would cost him his life behind bars. Wow, man, we were talking a couple of hours beforehand. Now, this was unbelievable, and I was in denial, not my friend or guy. Today he's still serving thirty-six years behind bars, and we talk from time to time as he stays in good spirits, trying to survive and live the best way he knows back there. If you don't know by now, my brother, I don't hate you for your choices. Yet, I love you because you were one of our brothers coming up through the ranks, and I wish you would've stopped and thought about what you would do before the devil took over you. That one bad choice could cost you your life because of your action. I love you, my brother, and I will always be here for you. Meanwhile, in Texas, numerous altercations would break out in the club, leading to guns being drowned due to us being intoxicated. We rolled deep, about twenty of us, quickly developing a name for ourselves as "We dem boyz" around Killeen, TX. Popular, young, and highly respected, what more could you ask for at the time? Unfortunately, we were soldiers. Just like that, the same hood life I was accustomed to was following me into the U.S Army; I mean, what if my car was to get stopped one day at the gate to do a random inspection which happened all the time, and those pistols were found in the cravats of my trunk being underage it would've been over for me. We were always trying to outsmart the system by only using gates that we were cool with people that worked them at, but that wasn't always the case. I was heading down the wrong path quickly; so many nights, things could have gone differently, and I needed to get my act together quickly.

A year had passed, and now we were in 2015. I was a few months from my first deployment to Kuwait and still getting loaded full of that liquor, doing what I thought was living life.

One night, while leaving my boy's house intoxicated, my homeboy started talking about racing. It's a narrow street and not to mention houses on both sides of the road, and before you know it, he was taking off in his car, and I was falling behind him. Now, maybe I didn't imagine the road ending so fast and coming up on the stop sign because it suddenly seemed as though he was at a halt, and to avoid running into the back of him, maybe I thought I could dodge him will lead me smacked dead into a tree at; at least about fifty miles per hour. Someone saved me again because it didn't take long for me to come back to my car, jump out and take off and run back down the road to my homie's house, screaming our homeboy had just got into an accident. That's right, I was so stunned and out of it until I thought our homeboy was the one who hit the tree. My mouth was busted, and my forehead was leaking blood, leaving me with a scar that still appears somewhat until this day, a faint streak line to always reminds me of that night and my accident where I almost came face to face with death. I still have no idea how my cousins got my car out of that person's yard and back to my homie's house before calling it in or whatever they did. I remember looking in the mirror and thinking boy have I done it this time? My face is banged up. My homie rushed me to the hospital, but we were smart. We knew we couldn't go to the hospital on base, so we went right there to the emergency room off base to deal with civilians and civilian police if they came again, always trying to hide the double life I was living outside of uniform because truthfully without that uniform on I was becoming a knucklehead. It's just that when work was work, I handled business knew my job exceptionally well, and everyone loved me for that. I was the most innocent kid and the best soldier anyone could ask for. I guess I just felt like no one needed to know what I did in my free time. I knew very well how to separate the two. Arriving in the emergency room and getting to the back, I believe the story goes, a dog ran out in front of me. Still, the nurse knew we were lying and said, "You know, be careful about how much you're drinking, and don't drink and drive. She wasn't going to get me all fixed up and taken care of without the police involvement. I received stitches in my mouth and some more medical treatment, and I remember asking for more and more cartoon orange juice; the liquor running through my body had me dehydrated to the max. Once I safely made it back to my room the next morning, I had to call my platoon sergeant and let him know what was going on, I was stitched up, and for the next few weeks, I would be cleaning out my forehead with a white gauze patch on my forehead. Like always, he assured me he had my back and would take care of everything. I had nothing to worry about, and just like he promised, I returned to work, and everyone blamed the stupid dog for running out in front of me with no consequences of my own. Woah, such a close call and another one would bite the dust but did that slow me down? No, of course not. Who did we think we were the untouchables or something, and then it happened, a wake-up call that none of us would forget? In September 2015, just a few days into the month, we lost one of our best friends to a motorcycle accident in the military; we all were just a few weeks before I would leave for deployment to Kuwait. Now, amid things for most people, this would be the final straw. It would shake others and draw the line. For me, it was different, and if we're being honest, I don't know what it is about that place, Fort Hood, but it seems like bad things were always happening that would result in tragedies like there always was a dark cloud over that place. I mean, it was so bad that there was a big digital board at each entry gate that detailed the number of days without having any soldier's death, and if it got to a hundred days or something like that, the whole base would get a four-day off. Well, I can tell you I lived there for three years, and I've maybe seen one or two four days. Because of that, it never got too high, and that was unfortunate. Someone's heart around there was always heavy. Death usually has its phases of being initially in denial. You don't want to believe it's true, and more so, like, can someone wake you up from this bad dream? The loss of our friend is where it took me over the top drinking wise, now I was never diagnosed as being an alcoholic showing up to work drunk out of my mind, or anything like that, but I began to crave liquor. By this time, we had graduated to drinking Hennessey, that's right, no more of the cheap stuff. To someone who may read this one day that knew me back then, you're probably smiling and saying to yourself yes, he did love him some Hennessey. My sister-in-law still reminds me of a kickback party I threw at my house in Texas, and a video surfaced of me taking a 750-milliliter bottle turning it upside down, and drinking it like it was water. She still laughs about it to this day. "Bro, you remember you took that Hennessey bottle and drank it like that! Death! She would always say".

Hennessey was my daily addiction, and I did not need a doctor to tell me that I had a problem drinking Hennessey to sleep daily. An expensive habit and a dangerous one, you know, the kind where after a few shots, you begin to feel like you have superpowers; that's the one for me. I'll take this time to give my first deployment thanks because although I had no idea of what to expect my first time leaving the country with my loved ones and family being thousands of miles away. I can now say thank you because I needed a break from Texas, I was living like it was no tomorrow outside of the military, and that usually never ends well, and if you believe in luck, it eventually runs out. Kuwait was, well, let's say, hot, very hot, with the spring and summer months reaching 115-127 degrees Fahrenheit. It was no joke. Besides that, sleeping in an open tent, seeing occasional rats here and there, and, oh, being a part of my first sandstorm during the winter months, it was not half bad. I was overseas making a little more money with nothing to spend it on, so on top of missing my loved one's family and friends, I was ready to get back to the states and spend some money. I was twenty, and it was the most money I had seen in my life accumulating in my bank account. Something would take place in Kuwait that I can only thank him for being a part of my journey still today. There was a building on the base that was called the drop zone, nothing big but something to have small things to do if free time would permit, a couple of pool tables, regular tables for playing cards, and a few couches where they would host pool tournaments, spade tournaments, and different little games like corn hole and more. I'll never forget the first day of meeting Jay, my mentor. I'm from the South. My grandparents, aunties, and uncles played cards, spades to be exact, so of course, I was at the card table my partner and me from Alabama wanted in. We all know card games come with a little friendly trash talk, and that's exactly what they were doing, so I felt right home in my element. Jay was at the table with him and his partner; he was talking trash, and they were the kings of the table. Jay was a government contractor for Lockheed Martin, a company that's a big deal in the government contracting world of things. Everyone wanted to work for them, and Jay was running the logistics side of the house as the man in charge of a team in places like Turkey, Iraq, Kuwait, and more. So, boom Jay and this one sergeant in the military begin to go back and forth when suddenly the sergeant asks Jay your wife, don't get lonely with you being over here back and forth contracting. Oh boy, now this conversation would then take a turn stopping the whole game, and you could see the expression on Jay's face that the comment did not sit well with him. He replied, with I bet you had debt, don't you? Now I did not know at the first catch on where the conversation was going with the comment jay made back, but then he began to elaborate. My wife hasn't worked in fifteen years. Anything she wants, she goes to the store and buys it. When my daughter wants to travel, we put all the countries in a hat. She draws a name for whatever country it says we travel and vacate. He had the residual income from being a retired First Sergeant, and due to his sacrifices and going after what he wanted in life, he and his family could enjoy life. The sergeant tried to explain that he did not mean anything by his comment, just saying being away has to be hard. Jay quickly fired back. Well, aren't you deployed and away for that little check you making? It's the same thing. The sergeant had nothing left, apologizing, then getting up and leaving. I never got the chance to get on the table that night, but I waited around until Jay was done playing before asking if I could speak with him, so we went sat off in the distance to another table, and I began firing my questions at him. He was an older guy late forties, straight out of Chicago, but he could still run a two-mile like he was a teenager on the track team back in high school. I had to be honest with him up front. I wanted to know everything. How did you make it out? How did you become who you're today? What's the most money you've ever seen in your life? You retired. Why do you still choose to work? What all countries have you visited? What's your professional and educational background? My questions were coming off like rapid fire and an automatic AK47. He had no problem answering it all and knew I was intrigued by what he was talking about. He broke it all down, having a Master's in Business and retiring from the military. He even told me how he likes his grass cut when he walks outside his home and his hired crew that cuts his grass, which was a funny and different story. Before I knew it, it was 1 AM and 2 AM, and I had work in a few hours, but I did not care. This was the guy I needed to be standing next to. Rather I had to ride his coat tail to learn or jump in his back pocket. I was down for the cause. We exchanged contact information, and the rest was history. I was like the son he never had; our bond continued to grow as his lessons and advice continue today. I'm sure this will make him laugh and reminisce on our first conversation when he gets the chance to read this, as I'm sure he probably did not think I would still remember that from many years ago, back in 2016. However, three things were clear to me after the initial conversation with Jay, education was important, and my goal was no longer a bachelor's degree but a master's degree. Two, residual passive income was a must, you could not work your way to wealth and financial freedom, and finally, sacrifices were tough but necessary to get where you're trying. His circle consisted of guys who lived the same way that he did. His employees own Bentleys, Cadillac Escalades, and all sorts of things, a quarter of a million dollars which seemed like a huge to me, was nothing for these guys. So, after nine months, we did return home safely, but things were a little different this time around. I still would drink a lot. That seemed to be the hardest thing to shake. Still, after seeing the money, I could make in nine months and having the conversation with my mentor Jay which was a lot at the time, being twenty and saving twenty thousand dollars in my bank account, a house with three cars in my driveway. I always knew growing up that I was fascinated with money. Still, at the age of twenty, the hunger I had begun to develop for it was different. Partying on the weekdays, then trying to get up to go to work, do PT, and go out in the clubs every weekend, was no longer my target. I began to deteriorate from those things cutting back what I thought tremendously, and in my free time, education became my focus. I would randomly research success stories of just ordinary people that live a lavish life today, what they have been through, where they started, what was the motivation behind it, and What was the fuel to their fire that fed their sensation that made them who they're today? Not always celebrities but just success stories. Knowledge was power, and today many people know me for that same motto as a few military awards. I have stated my favorite motto at the bottom "Knowledge is Power." I was like a shark who had just tasted blood. I needed some more to feed my sense of love for money and gain success, what I would call becoming somebody. I needed to do more, and the only way I could feed this money craving I had was to get more of it. During this time, money was probably my priority and what I cared about the most. This put distance between some of my friends, and truthfully speaking, some of them meant me no good anyway, so that was something I was willing to sacrifice. My pops were still in my head with my platoon sergeant and Jay still giving me advice and game, and now it was time for me to do something different I had to keep going; I was starting and blessed enough to have these guys in my corner who genuinely wanted to see me win. At the age of twenty, I will still make plenty of mistakes and decisions I'm not proud of because I'm only human right. I will still find myself drinking Hennessey with a mixture of red bull to hide the pain and various thoughts that would travel through my brain, later developing as anxiety. Meanwhile, back home in South Carolina, during my Kuwait tour, my hood had lost a legend, Dkelz. A real street dude who served a lengthy sentence but still had a heart of gold. Now, I didn't know how that worked, but I guess you can say that thugs also had a heart and were not always negative. We kept in contact from time to time, and even before joining the military, he was fresh home from prison, and I was a part of his workout regimen fitness group, which helped me prepare for the military. He would always say things like, "you a soldier boy," but not in the sense of being in the military but more so just being a solid kid at the time. He gave me my props and was always quick to assure me he was proud of me for going off and doing my thing, joining the military, and achieving everything I said I would without falling victim to the judicial system. He knew I respected him not solely based on his street credibility but on his person. He handled business, went to war with the best of them, survived shootouts, prisons, and more, and to lose him so soon shook the hood leaving everyone devastated. He was like the general, and I recall him saying, "every time we had beef with them niggas, I was always on the front line ready to ride" that was him behind loyalty. If he loved you, he would give his last, and any problem you had, he was going to go out of his way to make it his own. He was a hustler, a barber, and a gangster and family man all in one, but no stranger to who the man up above was and his faith. He kept a big dope boy knot in his pocket and was still loved by so many because everything about him was not always so bad. Do you remember my best friend snakehead well? He had fine himself back into some trouble again and was headed to prison for the next six months, and through it all, we always remained close. I mean, he could use the phone more than a little bit. I made sure to help keep money on his books because he was just a genuine friend. I remember him saying he was never going back to prison unless he had to behind his family, that it was not a place for humans. Some of the things he had seen in there and even getting into an altercation with a gang, I believe, bloods who, after he got the best of a guy, jumped him. With all of this still taking place in my life, it's like I still had one foot in and one foot out, but this was, in fact, the start of my transition. I've even had friends tell me that I valued money over everything else and that money wasn't everything. Here we go thinking of God for growth again because later in life, I understood that there's nothing wrong with being a Hustler. Still, it desires to balance, and money is, in fact, not everything and should never be prioritized over loved ones, but for now, Markus back then was not trying to feel that. Who would have me if I did not have myself? Besides, just like a shark who's tasted blood, what do you want it to do? Stop eating at that moment and understand why this is dangerous. No, not at all. No way, then you just might become prey. This would lead to my next move in my military career, coming down on orders for a permanent change of duty station to South Korea, Camp Humphreys. Huh? South Korea? Out of all the bases stateside, why would I be going there? This is the best you guys could do for me. I was only back in America for a year and a couple of months, and it was time to go again already, welp that was fast, which brings me to January of 2018, touching down in South Korea all alone and off to a new duty station for a year. I took this tour for two reasons. Serving this time overseas, I would get Fort Bragg, in Fayetteville, North Carolina, as my next duty station being just two hours from my hometown in South Carolina, so of course, I thought that would be cool. Then, of course, finally, for the money, I knew the extra compensation I would get for spending a year there. Man, oh man, did money influence many of my decisions back then. Fun fact: In the Korean age, everyone is already one year old at birth, and not only that: on New Year's, everyone simultaneously turns a year older! That means, in turn, you could be already two years older than you are in an international age. South Korea was amazing for the experience and helped me expand my mind on other cultures, and I loved it. Food is the essence of everything in Korea, and the city of Seoul is where you can find everything. You're looking for the high-rise mall with designer stores and beautiful views, even when it comes down to the food of their culture, their famous dish Kimchi, and their flavored barbecue meats. Koreans were big on culture and respected rules, so it was best you abide by them. However, we can't mention Korea without mentioning their nightlife, with club octagon being ranked internationally as one of the best clubs to party at in Asia along with their famous alcoholic beverage Soju, being one of the world's best-selling alcohols for years making Korean's one of the world's biggest consumers of hard liquor. As for me, Korea was the opposite of Kuwait. It was so cold that when you stepped outside, your hands would ache in pain from being so cold before eventually going numb. Do you know the feeling of being so cold? Better yet, let's say you have ever been so cold that if you hit your hand or finger up against something accidentally, it sends a striking pain through your nervous system, and you say to yourself, Ouch! Well, that was Korea in the winter months on top of dealing with the snow, but where I worked in the motor pool and flight line, it was not too bad of a walk daily from my barracks room, nope just cold with a running nose trying to stay warm but layers did not help, it was just that cold. My daily task consisted of monthly field exercises; we stayed in the field, being all over South Korea, Incheon, Busan, Osan, Camp Casey, you name it, we were all over that place. Even when North Korea was at the height of threatening nuclear warfare, the United States of America was there, and this was a scary time. Still, I did not overthink it but would always think well about the border, known as the Demilitarized zone (DMZ), which separates South Korea from its arch-enemy North Korea. I'm only sixty miles away from it, it could go down at any moment, but thankfully nothing ever took place. Still, peaceful protests throughout the village when units like mine, being aviation, would train, well our pilots would train flying our different aircraft, Blackhawks, chinooks, and more, and just like a weapons range, they would shoot off into the mountains their missiles for target practice, a very cool thing to see if you ever got the chance to experience something like it in person. That's right, South Korea was nothing but a big old bowl down in the middle and surrounded by the tallest mountains, so we kept a cold front. Well, these training exercises would sometimes disrupt the village, which sometimes led to small protests where we would have to stop training for a while. Enlisting as a Petroleum Supply Specialist but mainly always being on the aviation side of the house except for Fort Bragg. My career slightly differed from the average Petroleum Supply Specialist in a ground unit. I have always dealt with aircraft for the first five years of my career. Learning flight line and aviation fuel policies dos and don'ts. What it meant to test fuel daily in the lab with different testing equipment before being able to fuel a bird (aircraft). That was what we called parts per million, and it needed to stay below a certain number to be considered good fuel to go inside an aircraft. This was important because not knowing how to do your job could cost someone their life and you a long lengthy sentence at Fort Leavenworth, Missouri (military prison). This also came with documentation and accountant work, keeping track of your chain of custody, your daily, weekly, and monthly reports that were sent to a higher level in your chain of command, and most importantly, always, always, always, getting signatures so if worse came to worse you would be saving your ass. Work was always a breeze for me. I learned early on to master what I do or be good at it to the best of my ability. This helps you to stand out. Therefore, I'd like to say my team of soldiers who I supervised ran a tight ship, and even some to this day thank me and reminisce about the various things I taught them about the military and not only that but just life in general and how it has made them successful in their careers. So, I guess now would be a good time to thank all my soldiers publicly for those I was able to help along the way, motivate and strive to be better, and share a different point of view. In a nutshell, that's how Korea went for me, trying to lead my soldiers by example, never enforcing anything on them that I would not do myself. They cleaned or took out the trash in the company. I was doing the same thing right along with them. In my free time, however, I did enjoy going out to Incheon, a rather large casino, and sitting at the blackjack 21 tables for hours, playing in their currency, which is won, and then after a good night of gambling in the casino transferring the currency back over to USD currency. They also had soul food Thursdays in the cafeteria (DFAC) where you could get that soul food that many of us love, fried chicken, catfish, greens, white rice, mac and cheese, and more, with a plethora of desert selection to choose from so that was always nice. It did not taste half bad, making you feel at home with the Texas Pete hot sauce. I would return to the states in January of 2019 just as promised, with the duty station of my choice that I chose before leaving for Korea being Fort Bragg, North Carolina. When I thought I was safe and things were looking up for me, only within two weeks of being home, I would get the call that my battle buddy, another sergeant and good friend of mine, had committed suicide. We met in reception in Korea on our first day there and became good friends throughout our time in Korea for the year 2018 when we were in the same unit and platoon. He was an ammo specialist, and I was a petroleum specialist, so we were the first-line supervisors for our respective teams of soldiers in our platoon. When you're away from home, your battle buddies quickly grow on you as a family because we're all each other must depend on. The scars were piling up for me, and this one hit home. I vividly remember us hosting jeopardy in the classroom with the soldiers asking them questions about their jobs and army things like the soldier's creed and army song. If someone got it wrong, we would all do an exercise, a learning experience for the privates and specialists, but we also participated with them and made it fun so they would want to learn and understand that knowledge is, in fact, power. It's true what they say. You never know what a person is going through because Jack was funny, outgoing, and kept a smile on his face. You would have never seen it coming, not even in a million years. He was always too busy uplifting everyone else and encouraging those around him to be in good spirits. That's my point. That's what we might've missed. He hid his pain by encouraging us all to keep driving on through the hard times life brings with his silly jokes and laughter. Many times, he was my listening ear, and I wish before he decided to take his own life, he thought of me, picked up the phone, called, and I could've been his. You'll never be forgotten, my brother, as that platoon was something special, and we still hold on to the memories made with you forever. It wasn't too long after January 2019 that I would begin my transition of getting out of the

Army officially in April of 2020and, so that would become my focus and think of a masterplan on what I would do next with preparation. Me vs. Me chapter hit home and is where I began to make my transition into becoming a man with real responsibilities as a teenager and moving to Texas to serve my country at eighteenth, six and a half years later being twenty-four years old, in writing this chapter and taking myself down memory lane I got to see the bad choices I made, the things I was doing and what I learned from them, the childish state of mind I had to the maturity level I gained and is continuing on this journey we call life because no one is perfect. Most importantly, knowing that I now would not still make those same decisions I made back then or view life in that same light taking so many different things for granted and being proud of myself but understanding that those things I encountered even to include the alcoholic days, and all was who made me who I am today. I mean, if you never had to fall and get back up again, how would you ever know what growth and perseverance are like right. Here we go thanking God for growth again.

"I can because I'm capable, I will because I'm strong, I must because they're depending on me"

– Eric Thomas.

CHAPTER
7

EMOTIONAL ROLLERCOASTER

On December 12th, 2019, a cluster of patients was discovered in China, the city of Wuhan, experiencing symptoms of an atypical pneumonia-like illness that does not respond well to standard treatments. Cases began to slowly but surely break out in China. Initially, The World Health Organization believed this unknown pneumonia was in connection to the Huanan Seafood Wholesale Market, which was causing humans to encounter symptoms like shortness of breath and fever.

The World Health Organization closed The Huanan Seafood Wholesale Market to worries of another outbreak, such as the 2002-2004 Severe Acute Respiratory Syndrome Coronavirus or SARS-Cov-1 outbreak that took place in China. Meanwhile, back in America, of course, we were not paying much attention to what was going on in China; I mean, who wants to watch the news every day with all the propaganda involved? It's becoming a bit difficult to separate the truth from the lies. I watch the news from time to time to keep me aware of what's happening and not to seem like I'm just living under a rock. Little did we know over in the United States of America that an outbreak that was emerging in China was heading to the U.S. fast.

On January 20th, 2020, the Center For Diseases Control and Prevention (CDC) reported it was the first laboratory-confirmed case of the 2019 Novel Coronavirus in the U.S. from samples taken on January 18th in Washington state. The 2019-nCoV, later popularized as Covid 19 would hit the streets of America like The Mafia families, Bumpy Johnson, Nicky Barnes, Frank Lucas, Griselda Blanco, and more did the crack cocaine epidemic back in the 80's to the streets of Harlem up in New York. It spread like wildfire, and the most disheartening concern was that doctors did not have a discovery treatment for it at the time. I mean, they had seen nothing like it, almost as if it had fallen out of the sky, and bam, people were sick. From March 2020 to October 2021, Covid-19 was the third leading cause of death, one of the top five causes of death in every age group fifteen years or older. Covid-19 had a high target rate for those between the ages of 45-54 and 35-44 years old and grew enormously for elders aged 85 and older. At the time of writing this, according to the New York Times, The United States had reached 96.2 million cases with a total of 1.06 million deaths leading worldwide in cases and deaths, with California being the leading state with 11.3 million cases and 96,126 deaths.

Covid-19 has tallied up a scorching 618 million cases and 6.55 million deaths worldwide. Now, as you're reading this, you're probably thinking what I'm thinking and going wow, these numbers are insane and hard to believe but believe it's true. I mean, was it fair to the world that so many people lost their homes and career jobs, the working-class middle class and even the upper class? Banks tried to help push back due dates on payments, but it was too much to bear, and companies were going out of business quickly. Lifelong investments were being lost, businesses were being lost, homes were being foreclosed, and just when people were at the height of their careers, they were being let go due to the strain that the coronavirus had placed on the world. This did not make it any better in poverty areas because some of us already knew what it felt like to lose everything and have to start all over again, but this time was different. The world was getting a taste of its own medicine and the struggles some battle with daily. This was what it felt like to lose everything and, in the heat of the moment, feel like it's absolutely nothing you could do about it. This is what people were feeling globally, and it was at no fault of their own, and I can, for one, tell you that if Covid 19 was not a Permanent Scar, then I'm not sure what is. Was it fair? As the saying goes, life is unfair, so what will you do about it? Just quit and give up on your life? I mean, hey, it was Eric Thomas, my favorite motivational speaker, that said, "You're already in pain. Don't give up now. Get a reward for it", not me.

The world was on an emotional rollercoaster, an experience that alternates between making you feel excited, exhilarated, happy and sad, disappointed, or desperate. My nana caught covid twice and was in and out of the hospital, and both times, her life was spared for whatever reason the creator saw fit to do so. I still remember the conversation of her telling me in all her years of living, she had never seen anything like it, that diseases and outbreaks had occurred but nothing like this with this type of effect on the world, and that it was an unfortunate tragedy. She sounded so weak, and out of it on the phone, I felt like I was hurting her by actually calling to talk to her on the phone with tears in my eyes and a trembling voice. I just told her that I love her and that the hospital would take care of her and she would be just fine. The truth was that I could not stomach hearing my grandmother sound like that because she was always so healthy and energetic, always out in the yard doing something or moving around. Yup, she was always on the go, and to see the coronavirus come and have that effect on her just was too much for me, so I would keep in contact with my uncle and aunt on any updates until she returned home from the hospital safe and sound and was feeling like herself again. My nana wasn't alone, though. So far, I have never experienced being under the weather from Covid-19, and hopefully, it stays that way, but it did affect me. March 2020, on my way out the door on an honorable discharge from the Army, I had acquired over two months of leave days, so I could start my terminal leave a couple of months early from my official Expiration Time of Service date, which was April 21st, 2020. In February 2020, right before valentine's day, I had to sign the biggest offer letter of my life with a government agency, being a government contractor affiliated with the Airforce as a Fuel Expediter in Kuwait. Responsible for execution of 24/7/365 Base Operating Support Aircraft Fuels functions. Completing all aircraft, vehicle, maintenance, training, and other forms/documents required as part of an effective Aircraft Fuels Services program. Supervising subcontractors and your employees by also safeguarding all government property while ensuring all technical orders, publications, checklists, and forms are maintained as applicable. So, yes, my job consisted of things like that. The list goes on of what they don't tell you once your boots are on the ground. However, I was excited about my new future endeavors, and I had done it, just like Jay. I became a government contractor after the military, a path popularized by retired military and those who discharge honorably to go into government contract work. Why? For starters, you would remain on the federal side of the house for work. You still had the fundamental structure that the military gives and working with the military, so you were not a civilian but a government contractor. Finally, the reason that helps most people make the decision is their love for money. Since being tax-free and exempt from working in the country, it was too easy to double or triple your military salary income in nine months to a year if you did it right. This was military folks' outlet for trying to take a contracting job overseas to get ahead, which was, in fact, mine. Well, Covid, in the beginning, had other plans for me.

My timeline was set up perfectly. Two days out of the Army, I would fly to Kuwait to start my second job. I did not need a break; I needed to get to work and take advantage of this opportunity. Well, the day before leaving, more outbreaking news would surface, and the world, especially the United States of America, would mandate shutdown. Planes aren't flying. Flights are canceled. Stores are closing, and you must stay in your home. Remember that emotional rollercoaster that the world was in? Well, this news escalated emotions and sent the world into an uproar. Stores were running out of food, cleaning supplies, and much more. So, you mean to tell me I cannot go outside? Who was used to that? Schools aren't schooling anymore. Who was used to that? This sparked the viral moment of Covid babies sitting home daily, and people were out of jobs anyway, so it was best to get comfortable. Did this cause an educational disconnect in the Covid baby area? Well, I'm not sure, but I do know that the direction of the world was turning did not seem right at all. I mean, wearing a mask, and going anywhere, is required to take a covid test to enter somewhere. I do not know if I was more afraid of the disease or walking around and seeing all these people in masks covering half of their faces.

March 19th, 2020, a nice sunny Thursday with clear blue skies, was my last day in an Army uniform. Then, the next day March 20th, I would be celebrating my last day in America for a while, getting to make another trip overseas for the love of money and with plans of getting ahead financially in life. Well, not so face said the coronavirus and the memory still stuck in my membrane the world would shut down in a state of emergency on March 20th, 2020. No more flights and this would delay my process of getting overseas for another five months up until September of 2020 under one condition, changing my location from Kuwait to Afghanistan, which was where essential employees for government contracting were taking offers because the Kuwaiti government was not bulging essential workers or not no one was getting in that country in our out. Two things were for certain about changing my location to Afghanistan; I would make more because of being in a hazardous danger zone, and I would save more because, unlike Kuwait, where you can travel to the nice city and the beaches with various malls, I would be smack dead in the middle of the desert where your best view is just like being in South Korea like a bowl all you see is mountains off into the distance. Tall mountains surrounded you, and in the winter, they would be covered in snow and the whitest they could be. I remember always wondering Taliban would be looking at me right now, ready to blow my head off with some missile. These are the kind of thoughts that always run through one's mind in a hazardous zone. I mean, I had been to Iraq, but still, it was not Afghanistan. Over there Taliban got it cracking! And truthfully, I did not want any parts. So, what did I do? Well, I got on a plane, putting my life in danger, but I understood the risk, and it was optional. It was not forced, and besides, for those five months, we were being paid weekly to sit at home, but that would get old quickly. I was not a fan of just sitting around and felt like I was getting complacent and being trapped, you know, the crabs in the bucket mythology. I understood the risk, but I also understood the direction I wanted my life to go in, and the military lifestyle was pretty much all I knew.

I wasn't sure how to be a civilian again because, honestly speaking, after graduation four months later and at eighteen, I was in Basic training and never looked back. So did I even know what being a civilian was like? No. This was part of my plan for achieving the things I wanted in life; this was my foundation for building wealth that would help set me apart, and of course, for the love of money, I was chasing a different tax bracket. So, then I was off to Qatar, spending fourteen days in quarantine before we could fly into Afghanistan as a prerequisite. These were the two locations, either Qatar or Dubai, you would be flown to do your fourteen-day quarantine. I remember landing, getting off the plane, and then feeling like I could not breathe. It's like the heat of Qatar suffocates you, and although I was from the south, if you know you know, overseas heat is much different. Daily, someone would come to your room to check your temperature and take down any signs or symptoms of Covid-19. The food in the cafeteria (DFAC) was not bad either, and in every defeat, I would just like basic training. Look for that French breakfast toast with syrup that I knew would hit the spot. After my short jail sentence of being locked in a room pretty much for fourteen days was over, we would pack up and head down to Afghanistan. Entry to these hot zone countries was always pretty cool but a bit scary at the same time; you always fly in and land at night, and you can tell when we have just entered the country. The lights and everything go dark, from the cabins to the outside lights of the aircraft, so of course, enemies could not see that eye in the sky; night visions would permit us to see them, but unless they had some high technology infrared, we were in fact ghost's in the sky. This process was familiar as it was the standard operating procedure. I had done the same on my first deployment out of the country to Kuwait, where I also went to Iraq mid-tour with my M4, combat vest, and helmet with my magazines locked and loaded, ready for what could be coming our way. Now, I did not realize that these moments as such were causing PTSD with high anxiety, and the Army did not make it any better with the Candance calling songs that would get stuck in our heads during marches or five-mile runs.

"1,2,3,4 Hey, 1,2 give me some more hey, C-130 rolling down the strip, sixty-four trooper on a one-way trip, mission top secret destination unknown, they don't even know if they're coming home, stand-up hook-up shuffle to the door, we're going to jump right out on a count to four if my main don't open wide, I got a reserve by my side, if that one shall fail me too, look out down below I'm coming through, hit the ground in the middle of the night, I jump right out to a firefight.1,2,3,4 hey, if I shall die in a combat zone, box me up and ship me home. Tell my mama I did my best, bury me in a set of dress blues and the leaning rest. Pin my medals upon my chest and tell my family I did my best".

This is just one of many cadences we would sing, but, in a sense, as you can see for yourself, it made you wonder, will I die? This was not a call of duty, and you could reset the game and give it another try. This was real, and this is a part of what you signed up for on that dotted line and not v6 Camaros, Dodge Challenger, and Chargers, like some seem to think. See, mentally, in those deserts' reality would set in, and every morning was a blessing. Still, you had no choice but to think once the entry procedures to landing in these countries would today be my day. Would the Taliban be staring me in the eye and knocking the bird right out of the sky with the launch of a missile? A C-130, also known as The Lockheed C-130 Super Hercules Airforce military aircraft, is used to transport cargo, vehicles, and passengers. Remember Lockheed Martin Jay worked for? Everyone wanted to transition out of the military and get to work for a cool company like that; this was their design. They were always building and architecting cool things as a government agency company. So, now that you know what a C-130 is, to someone who may read this one day, you might've seen a picture of me surface years ago when I was twenty. I headed down into Iraq on the back of a C-130 with my vest on and M4 locked and loaded across my lap. Now, back in Afghanistan, we landed and met with one of the supervisors waiting for our arrival. He oversaw the night shift crew, which I would be replacing as he would move over to another position, still working in the same building, just a different department. Well, it's time to settle in. This would be my home for the next 12 months. We slept in the old barracks room surrounded by tall cement T-walls just in case we did receive incoming. Hopefully, it would hit the T-wall. First, all buildings, including the DFAC, were surrounded by the T-walls for the most part. I did have a roommate, but we would organize our wall locker closets to where we could not see each other, and besides he was on day shift, we would never be in the room simultaneously. Eventually, after about four months, he would move to his room. I knew how deployments went, and so I jumped right back into my normal schedule of being overseas time to lock in. Where are all the gym gurus? That's what you did overseas meet friends that love working out, and there it went day in and day out wake up to the gym, work, gym, then sleep, do it all over again, and of course, catch the DFAC for breakfast lunch dinner, and midnight chow. The DFAC on deployments overseas were always open 24/7 because of the various schedules the bases were on, and besides, operations overseas did not stop. It was 24/7; you would be surprised if you got a day off. Would you believe me if I told you from October 2020 to February 2021, I worked every day for sixteen hours a day, and then finally, I almost died from the lack of rest, and my body gave out. Well, okay, okay, that's not quite what happened. Still, my body did give out, and on top of that, our normal schedule was only required to work ten-hour days with one day off a week, and work was slowing up because President Biden promised to leave Afghanistan completely this same year. Before this came about, the crew I was in charge of had it down to a science sleep for four hours, get up, work out, and come back to get ready for work. Then, we had some workout equipment at work to work out there. Then after work, we would do a quick workout at the main gym again. Wow, now that I think about it, that was doing too much, but I was seeing gains and, at the time, the strongest I had ever been in my entire life. Then, eventually, working that many hours of overtime was not needed anymore, but we were still permitted to work twelve hours, so that I would do that. I mean, I was, what, twenty-five years old making anywhere from $4200-

4500 every two weeks tax-free on top of a monthly one-thousand-dollar bonus that they gave every employee that was considered to be a coronavirus bonus for Covid-19 working during covid, so that was an incentive and also receiving $2500 bonus for seasonal holidays like winter Christmas holiday, I mean I had never seen anything like it, I was feeding that starvation of a hustlers ambition to want more to get more money and in nine months I had made anywhere from one hundred five thousand to one hundred ten thousand and the best part about it was it was tax-free. I was stuck in a desert with no bills living and eating for free with nothing to spend my money on, which is a huge difference between tax-free and tax money. This means that a hundred thousand in America may be more like seventy thousand after taxes and your daily spending and bills. This brings me to my point about the holidays, this was the Taliban's favorite time of the year, and on holidays they were always trying to catch a body and hit the base. Until Christmas and New Year, we would always hear incoming sirens and things of that nature going off. Where most of us instead ran to the bunker-like, we were supposed to. If we were in our room trying to sleep, we would ignore the sirens roll over and try and sleep through it, praying to God the base is not being overrun. No bombs hit my room and killed me because we would eventually get used to things that were going to happen around us; it was a fate that everyone grew to accept capturing firefights on videos, bombs landing and blowing things up, and more.

New Year was different but expected because of intel that we knew we were hoping to get hit big this night and guess who was at work? Yes, of course, I was, and not to mention that the previous year before making it to Afghanistan, the base was breached, and a massive firefight with terrorists broke out as people ran and scrambled for their lives; people lost their lives, and buildings were destroyed to include parts of the hospital. Yup, that's right, so, call rigid bodies back in America or constantly talking about what they would do in a time of this or that but quite frankly, they have no idea; it's different when someone is trying to kill you with no consequences that will come behind it and not to mention an employee beforehand had scrape metal from the debris of a bomb strike come through the window of his fuel truck flying over to the airfield. Fun fact: It's never the bomb impact that mainly kills people but the sharp scrape metal that is flying around from the impact at high speeds that does, so its best to do as instructed, hit the ground and cover your head, and try to make it to the nearest bunker which is located all over the base. This would cause a permanent scar on this man for life, and he would immediately have to be sent on a flight home from out there. Where were we? New Year's night, that's right, and so it began one missile launch after the other Taliban was, in fact, this night, letting us know that they were trying to catch a body.

The Counter rocket, artillery, and mortar, C-RAM, that we had all over the base was a set of systems used to detect and destroy incoming rockets, artillery, and mortar rounds in the air from the enemy before they would hit the ground target. Still, they were coming in this night so rapidly that C-RAM could not catch them all. Thankfully to my knowledge, no one got injured or even killed, but the pain of being in the bunker for hours all night was tough enough. Remember, just like Korea being surrounded by the high rise mountains, it was freezing at 20 degrees Fahrenheit and below, and sometimes cold spells with 5-degree weather. So what do you know, when the incoming began? We all would hit the ground in the building for a few seconds covering our heads, then hopping up and booking it outside, making our way to the bunker with only the thought of safety being on our mind, so most of us were, in fact in the bunker without a jacket, a cover beanie or anything and we would be paying for it. This was a night I could never forget the C-RAM going off all night and mortar rounds and rockets landing here, ringing off in the distance, man. Was this somewhere I wanted to be? Am I seeing this with my own two eyes right now?

I was a long way from South Carolina, and they had no idea what I was experiencing and going through. Not to mention the streets I know back home, my community constantly lost people. But, unfortunately, that would never come to an end. I remember after that night in January. Reality would begin to set in. It was not about the money anymore, and just once before, as stated, my friend was right. I put money before everything, and I did now in a situation and place I no longer wanted to be in. Now, it's fair to mention that overseas contracts can be broken.

It's no obligation to fulfill my time there, so I could leave whenever I wanted to, but a little pride would not allow me to. I was still willing to take that risk until May, just two weeks before my birthday, May 18th. By this time, I was just torn; the same oh routine, only going four places for the past nine months, had just gotten old with the DFAC, work, barracks room, and gym. I was going crazy; I felt tired of it all being locked caged inside a box I felt like. I was around a bunch of men daily with testosterone, and things were getting unpleasant for me. I started feeling like higher-ups were controlling me and wanted me to do something they saw fit and not what was most beneficial for the employees. I was far from new to running a team of soldiers or employees, ten to fifteen at a time, ranking early in the Army as a noncommissioned officer. I had already developed my leadership style, and I took pride in knowing that anyone under my squad could say they learned something from me. It was difficult to lead the way others thought I should, and to be honest, most higher ranks would often forget the process of working their way up through the ranks losing that touch with the lower level that I still had. If I was being honest, I began to develop hate for the leadership there. To me, it was toxic men in control that were probably nobodies growing up getting some power and authority and just running away with it. So for one, I was just over it, risking my life daily for what I would begin to feel like. Anyone knowing me knows that I strongly dislike the word hate, and it was not until recently, in the year 2022, that I developed so much hatred for the way they to me treated people that I was able to let it all go.

Finally, I remember feeling like these people had to be dealt with if we ever ran into them in America. I had to represent people who were afraid and did not have legs to stand on. It would hit me this particular night in the late days of April that we were assigned. I would see a mini ceremony of caskets wrapped in an American flag being loaded in the back of a C-130, and the people standing out seeing them off were crushed. I mean, you could see the looks on their face. They wanted out just like me. Enough was enough, and to make matters worse, every day in the news, the U.S. government was going back and forth with terrorists and their miraculous threats as if we weren't out of Afghanistan in the matter of the next few months' deadlines. It would be hell to pay and more bloodshed. Now, if you know anything about terrorists, they weren't bluffing, and how did you guys have all these means to reach over government anyway? What's going on in the background?

Well, maybe that's another story for another day or book. Taliban are, let's say, crazy as hell; I mean, you believe in your culture so much that you're willing to wear a suicide bomber jacket that will take your own life and mine. You hate Americans so much that you eat, sleep, breathe, kill, wanting to kill Americans. No way; this has got to be unbelievable, right? Well, that was all true. Rather if it was by choice or not, that's the life they lived, and I knew what it was like to see fifty black robes and dressed personnel with the Taliban flag flying high and pride march. Compliments from my first deployment in Kuwait, where I was in an unmanned drone unit, we could see everything from the eye in the sky. Once in Iraq, a suicide bomber would try to run his vehicle through the gate, but he was shown dead before approaching the gate in marines over at Camp Al Asad. Then again, in Afghanistan where a suicide bomber did get on base but was discovered and stopped by a First Sergeant. This First Sergeant lost his life as the bomber got scared and triggered the button. Still, he did save the lives of hundreds of people who were gathered on this particular day for a holiday run around the base where the suicide bomber was headed. Hats off to you, top one of our heroes. May your legacy live on.

All of this was compiled. Finally, I could not take it anymore. I felt lonely, my mother was going through a divorce and in pain, and that's something I could not just take the pain away from. I felt neglected and forgotten by so many people and loved ones who I thought were supposed to be there checking on me. This night I sat in that truck, and I cried. I cried like a baby. Once the tears started, it was an overflow with Kirk Franklin melodies from heaven and Marvin Sapp *The Best in Me* repeatedly playing in the background from my phone.

The tears were slowly drying up, and as I was getting myself together, I would reach my grandmother, my mother's mom, and explain to her what was going on and that I honestly was losing myself. This deployment was breaking me. I did not want to be strong anymore. This wasn't normal. This is not how people should live, with random blackouts and being secluded from the world. She prayed over me and said you know who God is, don't you? I replied, with I do and from there, she assured me everything would be alright. Just hold on and keep my faith even when you are being battle tested.

Shortly after this conversation, a week later, I would drop my leave packet to go home for a few weeks, stop in Dubai then make my way back to America on May 2nd, 2021. I was out of there, and in the back of my mind, I was assured that if my feet made it back to United states soil, Afghanistan would be a place I would never wish to return to. Fun fact: In the 1970s, cities in Afghanistan like Kabul was a glorious and beautiful tourist destination. Over 90,000 tourists would travel to the country of Afghanistan to experience the culture of the people and its fine fruits and see the country's unique beauty, but the Taliban would later destroy this. To my surprise June our contract would be forced politically under government regulation to end anyway due to America holding up their end of the bargain. President Biden would declare all military, staff, contractors, and entities to leave Afghanistan. So from there, I would think, well, I would have hated to be the last few hundred people leaving that place anyway but wait, there's more of a catch-22. Leaving out of Bagram, Afghanistan, the biggest, I'd say, one of the safer locations to be in Afghanistan if you ever go there. Still, we had to stop in Kandahar, and everyone on that flight hated it, questioning why we needed to stop here for fuel at this flight base when we had just left Bagram 30 minutes ago. Kandahar was dangerous, and the villages were right outside of the base. You could reach your hand over the gates and touch the other side. We were that close, and this was not okay.

Fueling the aircraft consisted of everyone getting off the flight, and we would be locked in a building for over an hour. People were panicking. I remember people saying things like, "It's no way I made it this close to making it out of Afghanistan then landing in Kandahar to die because we were literally that close and the NATO and action now operated Kandahar could pop off at any given moment everyone was anxious to get to their respective destination and little did we know things like this was doing nothing but adding fuel to the anxiety fire and PTSD. We eventually boarded our flight, and everyone would, to my knowledge, make it safely to their destination. Being away for nine months and pretty much secluded, I guess I did not have much time to consider the world being, in fact, still in a pandemic, and things were still far from normal. The world was still, in fact, on an emotional rollercoaster, and the permanent scars of constantly running my blood pressure up in Afghanistan daily, thinking, will I die today? So was I, an emotional rollercoaster.

"The ultimate measure of a man is not where he stands in moments of comfort and convenience, but where he stands at times of challenge and controversy"

- Martin Luther King Jr.

CHAPTER

8

HIDDEN TEARS

Before you knew it, I was back in that South Carolina summer of 2021 with humidity and heat. I remember the plane ride from Dubai to New York like yesterday. Man, we were going through a rocky state, and the turbulence gave our flight the business. Now, if you have ever been on a plane and experienced that segment of bad turmoil, then you know exactly what I'm talking about. The bell ding goes off in the cabin, inquiring you to put your seat belts on, and all I could think was, "Lord, you've brought me too far to let me go out like this" while the plane is rocking doing its turbulence dance and I'm sweating bullets inside of my Afghanistan black hoodie.

Does anyone else like flying because it's the most convenient but dislike it simultaneously? Well, that's me, and even though I've gotten better since I was a kid, sometimes motion sickness still creeps up on me when it wants to with a mixture of nausea and, let me tell you, on a flight way up in the sky this does not go well when your anxiety is also climbing through the roof due to turbulence. On the other hand, I love the calm, cool, and collected flights where I can nap peacefully. After all, I would make it back to The United States of America safe and sound where for that summer, May, June, and July, I would spend most of my time in South Carolina back in my hood Oatland also known as part of our tri-area route 4. I quickly discovered something was missing, and I felt out of place. I have never stopped going to school, taking online classes at the University of Maryland since August 2014. This fall of 2021, I will graduate with my Master of Cybersecurity Technology. Fun fact: I have an associate degree in General Studies, a bachelor's degree in Business Administration, graduate school certification in Cybersecurity, and lastly, my master's degree in Cybersecurity technology, and I've never been on a college campus, let online walked a college stage. However, I 'am an alumnus of the University of Maryland and a member of the Upsilon Pi Epsilon of college honor societies.

UPE is an international Honor society for computing and information discipline for academic excellence. Even with all these accolades that I should've been proud of, I was not. I used to say that I eventually enrolled online to further my education because it was the traditional American Dream way. It was not until recently, in 2022, that I would reap the benefits of having an educational background and the rooms it would put me in. Meanwhile, back during this time in South Carolina, I mainly just wanted to fit back in with everyone that I was around. Being from the country, we mainly have our way of living, our own culture, that the world knows nothing about, which makes big cities a culture shock. Life is much slower in the country, and most will never experience life outside of that. Is it a bad thing? Not but it's just a life that sometimes we as country folks grow accustomed to too. I remember my big bro Jeff who is like family to me, would land his first huge job with Microsoft out in Seattle, Washington. Coincidently, this was a city I was quite familiar with because my mother was stationed at Fort Lewis, Washington. He would later land in Houston and transition to working for Apple as a Global Supply Manager. He always tried to tell me about the rooms he was entering, the people he was meeting, and his vision of the great benefits life had to offer once you stepped outside the box of the traditional thinking of what you're used to. I always heard him out in conversations and knew what he meant, but it just didn't seem to be me at the time, others saw me in that light, but I didn't see myself there. It wasn't until my vacation to Houston in the year 2022 that we reconnected face to face, and I got to see the experience for myself and the deep intellectual conversations we would always talk about. His and his wife's lifestyle was just different, they had balance, and you could see the hard work put in to get where they were. This was when the light bulb would go off for me, step outside the box, networking is power, work hard, and dream big; it was all coming full circle for me. Although we both struggled with not wanting to feel like we were neglecting anyone back home and forgetting where we came from, we also understood the bigger picture. This was what would ride my back the summer of 2021; I guess I was trying to fit in when certain things, just me, were not anymore. I was fresh from Afghanistan, with thousands of dollars in my bank account, and making another contract or going job hunting was the furthest thing from my mind. Who remembers the day they bought their car? Well, I remember passing Georgetown Auto Sales in Georgetown, SC, and seeing the new white GMC Sierra lifted truck on mud tires and nice rims. Turning at the light, it was almost love at first sight, and I just had to pull into the dealership to see it. Were my eyes playing tricks on me, or was this the one? A rep for the dealership would come out with the keys and let me take it for a drive and check out the inside, giving me all the details and information, I needed to know. It was white, my favorite and the only color for any vehicle that I would own, but the only problem was I did not care for trucks. I mean, I wasn't tall, 5'7 on a good day, and I only wanted one because of the stereotype all men need a truck. As the old saying goes, the money was burning a hole in my pocket. I returned the same day with fifteen thousand cash as a down payment and drove off the lot in my brand-new GMC Sierra, and I loved it. Still, up until this day, it mainly collects dust, so I guess the whole point of the purchase was simply because of the saying, all men need a truck. Besides that, being my biggest purchase for my twenty-six birthday, I did not even do too much shopping; most of my time was spent at the racetrack with motorcycles on the weekends or late-night car street races. I would develop the love for shooting dice the quickest way I would ever make a couple of hundreds or a couple of thousands. Not to toot my own horn, but shooting dice was something I was good at from the summer of 2020 until the summer of 2021; that was my year of addiction; I had to shoot dice. I could count on one hand anytime I've taken a loss worth talking about in gambling. Most people would say gambling is a 50/50 percent chance of winning, but it's not. Some people are wise gamblers and know how to gamble; some people are better at it than others, and if you're into gambling on football, basketball sports games, racing, shooting dice, or Poole. You know exactly what I'm talking about. Trust me, if that was me, I'm quite sure I could live off it without a doubt in my mind, no problem. Who was I kidding, though, this would slowly come to an end for me, and it was boring, honestly speaking, waking up doing the same thing every day, and those with jobs were at work. Man, how do some people sit around daily with nothing to do? This wasn't an easy task, and I struggled to find my niche of not being in the military.

After six and half years of serving my country in uniform and then transitioning to another uniform as a government contractor, that lifestyle that I struggled with is what I still gravitated towards and needed in my life. It was tough trying to detach as a civilian. I still remember days of being home back in South Carolina and some retail or food stores not offering a military discount. This was all so new to me, and being biased, of course, I would think, "Well, that's dumb. What store doesn't offer a military discount." I mean, are you serious?

In my head, it was definitely like two worlds out here, and that check on the first and fifteen was not automatically depositing regardless of if I went to work or not, unlike the luxury of the military. Hmm, was, in fact, the structurally designed system of the military a weight lifted off your shoulders compared to civilians? I mean, the military percentage only made up one percent of the American population, so maybe not, or maybe some did not have the courage or fear of taking that step into that room, raising their right hand, and taking on that military oath to defend their country at all cost. Whatever the reason was, this thought would always race through my mind in the beginning if I had made a mistake because, as stated before, the Army naturally came easy to me.

Everything was in black and white, no matter the rank you were in or the position you held. Then, boom, one night, it hit me. Those hidden tears would soon become tears sitting in my grandmother's house in one of the bedrooms feeling so lost yet overwhelmed. What was I doing with myself? Had I come this far to whine up back where it all started? This gut feeling did not feel so well at all, I had lost myself, and it was like I was in the middle of a crossroads, and I did not know rather go left or right; I had college degrees but did not even know how to start to put them to use. I mean, what's a resume? I'm a military brat. I never needed one of those, and what goes on a resume anyway; keywords, skills, or what? So, I did the one thing I always knew how to do and was good at, wipe the tears out my eyes, grab some tissue blow the snot out my nose, open my notebook, grab a ballpoint pen, and get to playing with numbers writing down different ideas I could pursue and what was next for me. Okay, here's my bank account. You have this amount, and according to my bank account statements, this is my average daily spending minus my bills, and this is what it takes for me to survive a month.

This is the magic number I need in income a month to survive and live the life that I was accustomed to; ole boy flipping fries at McDonald's was not going to cut it. What was the one famous thing that most men in the country were known for? Big trucks! 18-wheelers, that's right, most of the people where I'm from drove trucks and hauled wood to the mill in the city of Georgetown. What did one of your friends who had become successful at it do for a living? Own a trucking company but ran over-the-road long haul freight with a flatbed trailer. Then it began the next day; that was it picking those who I felt would lead me in the right direction, brains because I was a student of the game; I needed to know the good, bad, and the ugly and not let back. I needed to know it all. Fun fact: When I'm intrigued by something, I ask many questions. If I was going to start my own trucking company, I needed to know exactly what to expect, and as for me, preferably the cons, so I knew what not to do the pros I could figure out with time. I dug into research and sat on YouTube for hours.

I wanted to know everything, from company owners to dispatchers, to brokers, rates per mile, how to seal contract freight for dedicated runs to keep your truck consistent, and the bills paid. The funny thing is, with all this research, I was missing the most critical piece to the puzzle. To my luck, this was not hard for me to find; well, remember my right-hand man, nickname snake? I gave him a call and pitched my idea, and after a good conversation, he was on board and completed the game. His girlfriend was almost due to have their little boy Milo, but after that, he was all in. So, bro, what are we going to call ourselves? Kid asked his friends in the movie Biker Boys when they were about to branch off and start their bike club. I would reply, All Gas, No Brakes Transports. Yea, that's it. That's what we're going to call ourselves. We both loved the name, and on July 1st, 2021, the company LLC was off to the races. Now once all our paperwork and meeting Department of Transportation guidelines was in order, we needed a Truck, and of course, that was his task to find.

I had no idea what I was looking for, let alone the best transmissions and motors to buy in an 18-wheeler. My knowledge and experience only went as far as what I had learned on YouTube. He didn't mind it anyway; most truckers are sleep-breathing trucks. It's all they care to talk about for the most part, and besides, he was hauling wood for a company for a couple of years now and just wanted to do something different, so he was all game. Before you knew it, we were in Miami, Florida, picking up my red Freightliner classic, an investment that cost me 30,000 dollars. I remember arriving, and the picture on Marketplace was not doing the inside of the truck any justice at all; the original wood grain floor and the steering wheel were so nice and profound that I liked it, yea not too bad, bro. You picked out a good one. It fired right up, and around Miami we went pulling gears and jumping on and off the jagged brakes creating that noise everyone loves to hear when 18-wheelers pass by, and so after that test drive, the man was paid in full cash, a Hispanic guy was who did not speak fluently and he English but his best friend. Before making our way to Miami, he had previously stressed on the phone that someone came from Detroit with 27,000 dollars cash, and he turned them around. It was unfortunate they came that far, but 30,000 was his price, and he was not budging as the motor in the Freightliner classic was just not freshly redone. I enjoyed this information and guy like this because, for one, it instantly told me without him saying so that we were going to purchase a good truck. He knew what he had, and that was that he needed 30,000 dollars, and for two, he could not be bought by just seeing that kind of money upfront in person; he was a man of dignity. I assured him 30,000 dollars was what we were coming with, and if the truck paperwork, maintenance, and so on would check out, that's the amount he would be receiving.

We returned safely to Georgetown, South Carolina, and at the beginning of August, with a freshly polished truck, it was game on and time to get rolling. For a couple of weeks, we ran locally, which still averaged good money, but we wanted more and knew it was more to be made; we led with the concept of taking advantage of the truck while it was fresh before any costly maintenance issues could occur if any for at least running strong and hard for the first six months. It did not take us long to get in with a nearby plant, American Gypsum hauling sheet rock up North to its Virginia and Maryland locations. This was when things got lovely, and trucking seemed like a piece of cake, and within five months, All Gas No Brakes Transports had broken into a six-figure revenue company by December of 2021. I mean, we were like Shaq and Kobe or, better yet, MJ and Scottie Pippen and averaged eighty-seven hundred dollars consistently on a normal week, and the money was flowing in. I would book the loads from the home of my residence in Tennessee, but it was nothing like the hours he would drive weekly and the hands-on physical labor of strapping down the freight. So, in short, those hidden tears were the start of a thriving trucking company to make its mark in the world as All Gas No Brakes Transports; I had found my niche outside of the U.S. military.

"Life will only change when you become more committed to your dreams than your comfort zone"

                                         – Bill Cox.

CHAPTER

9

APPLE OF MY EYE

Did you know that in the game of chess, the Queen chess piece is the most powerful chess piece on the board? Wow, even more, powerful than the King? Yes, even more, powerful than the king, and here's why. The story has it that Queen Isabella of Spain inspired the queen's chess piece. The Arabs introduced the game of chess in the 8th century to Spain during its invasion, but it was not until the late 15th century, when Queen Isabella was at the height of her powers, that the chess queen became the most powerful piece. Initially, when Isabella was crowned Queen of Castile, the figure could only move one square at a time, just like the King. Later, once Isabella became the most powerful woman in Europe, the present rules of chess were established where the Queen could move in all directions on the board; however, it saw fit to launch attacks, making it the most powerful chess piece on the board.

The meaning of Queen in the game of chess is the closes support to the King, being the ear of the King and providing advice signifying her power and importance and being known as the most fearsome member of the Army on the chess board. This had Queen B, my wife, and the Apple of my Eye written all over it. Apple of my eye was a clever nickname she had earned over the years, referring to in the English phrase as something or someone that one cherishes above all others or, as the old-fashioned term has it, the person who someone loves most and is very proud of. So, I guess here's the part of the story where I tell someone who may read this one day where it all began. Well, somewhere a long time ago, on one hot sunny June day out in Killeen, Texas, in 2015. My crew and I would always be out chilling at our homie's house, where he lived in a townhome, meaning he had a neighbor in the other multi-family home. Well, this night, me and the fellas were all out drinking outside the norm. I was fresh from a three-month training with my unit out in National Training Center, NTC the deserts of California, Fort Irwin, but being in an aviation unit, we got lucky, and our time was spent in these mobile type of trailer homes on Fort Edwards Airforce base where we could fly and land our aircraft. So, I was happy to be back in my element and environment. There she was, chilling at her home girl's house, sitting out on, I guess we can call it, a porch where her friend had a few chairs, and they were just over there talking it up, laughing it up about, I guess, women gossip. I knew her homegirl since she was in my homeboy neighborhood, but Brittney, nope, I had never laid eyes on her before. The reason was that she was down for the summer visiting her sister, who was also stationed at Fort Hood and had just had a newborn. She was attending Tennessee State University, majoring in Biology for her bachelor's degree. Coincidently, her parents had just left for Poland, where her father was stationed; he was also in the Army. Yes, a long line of military folk's backgrounds. Either way, by the end of the night, that alcohol was fully loaded and pumping through my bloodstream, and it was clear as day that I wanted to make her mine. I mean, not aggressively, but your intentions should be clear, right? Finally, she gave in and handed over the digits to her cell phone but being who my crew was. She probably had no intention of ever taking me seriously initially. Still, my mother always told me I have a way with words. As the weeks went by, with more and countless conversations and lunches, the attachment and emotions would begin to develop, and one night at a kickback we would throw at my homeboy's house, she would have just a little too much drink. I would find myself back in my barracks room, taking care of her all night to ensure that she was okay. I mean, the girl was wasted, you hear me?

In our barracks had the luxury of having our room and nice size walk-in closet through my room door would be the kitchen that I would have to share with one other person and the bathroom as well that took you out the kitchen doors to the other roommate's room but luckily I never had a roommate. Hence, even the kitchen and bathroom were all mine. After that night of taking care of Britt, she never left, and the rest was history; we started doing everything together. The clubs, the fourth of July fireworks show on base, and even my crazy drunk antics on 6th street out in Austin, Texas, she was there to witness it all. Oh man, embarrassing memories that are funny today and will last a lifetime. I remember driving from Austin,

Texas one night, in my white mustang, sitting on 24-inch rims with my left foot out the window the whole way back to Killeen; why? I don't know. I had just turned twenty and was not thinking straight. That's not all, though. In the beginning, she quickly showed that she genuinely loved the kid, and when I lost my friend to that motorcycle accident, I was devastated. Now the roles had flipped. It was her turn to take care of me that night and hold me in her arms until I was sound asleep.

September, I would be leaving for Kuwait just a few days before her birthday on the 28th. I ordered her a few pairs of sneakers and heels. Of course, the heels were all the wrong size, and we had to send them back for the correct size.

Going off to Kuwait for my first deployment, I expected to get played, used, and abused and eventually disappear like I was doing a lengthy ten-year prison sentence in the joint. However, what happened was quite the opposite. Conversations grew more profound, and connections grew stronger. So, is it true that distance makes the heart grow, founder? Well, I imagine so because that's what's beginning to happen. I was receiving the best care packages on the base, hands down, and everyone was jealous. I mean, she was sending so many things I could share with my squad if I chose boxes of honeybuns (I guess she caught on quickly how much I love honey buns) and boxes of candy for my sweet tooth. In addition, she was sending bundles of Dove soap and deodorant, hair products for my hair, I mean, you name it, anything that I loved or needed to survive, and this kept me going. I had never seen anything like it, this girl was the next best thing to perfect, and nothing short of amazing, and what I admired the most was that she wasn't a party animal.

Fun fact: For me, a turnoff is a woman who must be in the clubs partying every weekend. Enjoy stepping out from time to time to digest, but every weekend could be a bit much.

She had possession of my mustang and was taking care of my car. She had her car, but she was also taking care of mine. OMG, I THINK I'M IN LOVE! Before you know it, six months later, on December 28th, 2015, we were doing all this paperwork electronically and sending documents back and forth from overseas to be notarized with witnesses to seal the deal of marriage through video call. Call us crazy or two fools in love, but it felt right, so that's what we did and what do you know, this December 2022 makes seven years, so I guess you can say we were on to something. It's no way she was returning to Tennessee State University at this point. However, she did finish her bachelor's degree in Biology online.

I still remember the first video call with her parents. I was in Kuwait, and they were in Poland. It was a natural connection. Her father asked me questions and was concerned about the same thing any other father would be who just married their daughter. Her father and mother were both smooth, though. I guess they did not want to lead with any assumptions, but time would tell, and they made clear that although in the back of their mind, I'm sure they thought we were moving outrageously fast, they ensured we had their support and the same with my stepdad and mother when she spoke with them. Besides, I was in the Army and this is what people do they marry young. I mean, that's a little funny to say, but it's true. It is like the only stigma or stereotype the Army has that is true. Who wants to be locked up in the barracks when they've found love and could be reaping the benefits? It's time to start a life of my own. So, that's how the marriage happened for us, a top-tier wedding one day? I'm not sure, but we both agreed that the cost of the wedding we would have could be more beneficial using it elsewhere, you know, owning rental properties. I was whining down my deployment, and she was doing all the leg work to ensure I was coming back to a lovely home, and let me tell you, she went all out finding a beautiful two-story home in what I would say one of the best neighborhood's being Bridgewood that Killeen has to offer.

Fun fact: She furnished the whole place with her own money! Round of applause to the ladies that don't need their man just for their money; I could get used to this. I remember coming home after the ceremony on the calvary field, her running, flying, blowing, and jumping in my arms; I had never seen anything like it, another human being that excited and happy to see little whole me. It did not stop there; the house was filled with flowers, balloons, and rose petals which led to a nice warm candlelight bath of water for me to relax on my first day home. This was by far the sweetest thing a person had ever done for me, and we were off to the races of living our newlywed married life.

Well-experienced a lot together on our first trip to San Antonio for the weekend. The experience of the River Walk was highly recommended for anyone in Texas to visit. Our home eventually became a liked hangout spot for our friends, where we had Thanksgiving functions and other BBQ cookout events. My wife and I even spent our first Christmas together in that house, just us, one prominent place, and it was only the two of us; it was funny that year trying to guess each other's gifts and what we had gotten from one another having to wait for Christmas to unwrap them from under the tree. Most of us being miles and miles away from home, the people there we knew became family, and this was all we had. We threw some of the fattest kickback parties, and I remember that video I told you about that would surface that her sister always still brings up about me turning the 750ml bottle of Hennessey upside down and drinking it yea, that's where that took place. Our house is in the garage while playing beer pong and music. I was in my prime of drinking back then, and the Hennessey king, everyone would come over and have a ball with no altercations or wild nights leading up to disaster. This is how the three years of us living in Texas would go. We were both working and grinding our way through the ranks of furthering our education with college degrees. She was always tough on herself because her friends had graduated before, and she felt like she was falling behind. Being her husband, I always tried to keep her motivated with encouraging words, which did help, but this stayed with her in the back of her mind as she continued to pursue her medical field career; she just always knew that for herself and her accolades, she wanted more. It was bigger than just being a down wife and working a job, cooking, cleaning, and taking care of the house; it was so much more that she knew the world had to offer her. She was a down wife, too, so down that she was willing to risk her life along with mine.

Things escalate quickly, and she will very much so could have. Now, it's time for a story inside of a story. By now, you know that I was always into getting money no matter how it came. Even with being a U.S. soldier, I had a love for multiple streams of income; why? Because I was told that being a hard worker doesn't earn your way to wealth, investments and numerous income streams do. So, with that being said, let's say I was dealing with a group of guys I shouldn't have been doing things I should not have, and tonight is where things got real. At midnight my phone blew up, and it woke her first as she was tapping me to grab my phone; as I looked who was calling, it was these guys, and what I do? Ignore the car. I have formed in a few hours, and of course, they call back, and this time I answer. My guy is in a rage. Long story short, some money was tangled up, things were missing, and he wanted to get to the bottom of this.

After a few minutes of going back and forth, we decided we would meet inside Walmart at the back in the electronic department, a public location. Of course, he was brilliant, but I had a brain myself. My guys are on speed dial. Who was the middleman in the deal? He would be showing up as well the rest of our crew would act as regular shoppers in Walmart who they did not know but would be nearby just in case things left. As I was getting up and getting ready to meet, she started getting up and putting on her clothes and saying, "I'm going with you". Now, my response probably should have been women. Are you crazy? It's about to be twenty-thirty men inside Walmart, and at any given point, things could get out of hand but what came out of my mouth was okay. I mean, she didn't think twice about questioning me or anything. She just knew she was coming along and whatever it was going to be was what it would be. By this time, we had legally registered weapons all over the house, and I held my license to carry them. I mean, we had a couple of Glock's 9 millimeters, a pistol grip Mossberg pump that was loaded with slugs, an AK-47 that shot 7.62, an AR that fired 5.56, and a Sig Sauer .40 with a green dot that was sure to pick off any given target it was aimed at. My wife was no stranger to the gun range as she often went with me on the weekends to shoot the weapons for target practice, so she knew how to handle herself. Don't let the pretty face fool you.

So, we got to Walmart and instantly noticed the scene and a few ducked-off cars. Well, that was obvious. She parked, and I tucked two pistols in my pants while she had the Ak-47 lying across the back seat, said I love you, and then went inside. So soon as I made it through the doors, she knew to move out of the parking space and pull around the side and keep the car running. So, boom, there we all were in the back of Walmart, intense and alpha males with a lot of testosterone clutching and ready for what could break out to be a shootout if we weren't able to get to the bottom of this. Thankfully, this all ended well, and we were able to figure out the problem and that it was all a big misunderstanding. We all remained cool as things continued flowing, but I knew from that night moving forward, I was cutting business short it had come too close to home, and it was not that serious to me. I was already successful in the Army anyway. So a few weeks later, we would all be laughing at that night in Wal-Mart like a man that could have been bad for everyone, and what made us choose Wal-Mart was a crazy, not wise idea at all. Shortly after that, I would cut ties that they respected and never hear from those guys again; today, I could not even tell you, their names; I mean, I was twenty-one when this took place.

After three fun years in Texas, duty had called again, and this is where I spent the year 2018 in South Korea, then returning to Fort Bragg, North Carolina, in 2019. 2018 was our first time in Virginia

Beach, I came home for two weeks for her birthday on September 28th, and we spent her birthday in Virginia Beach. The most remarkable thing about the trip was the massive beach tent with the unique sand sculptures carved into so many different things. I mean, it was an amazing to work of art to see, and the seafood we would get served all night at the restaurant we would attend later that evening. Of course, I still had my Hennessy and coke, but after being in Korea and not drinking, I did not have it like I used to when it came down to drinking alcohol. I would return to Korea to finish my tour and return to Fort Bragg, North Carolina in January 2019. The following year I would be honorably discharging ETS and preparing for government contracting overseas. By this time, working in the medical field was alright, but as I stated, she wanted to do something different and gain more under her belt. I don't know. It was like something haunted her in the back of her mind.

I tried to talk her out of joining the military long enough when we initially got together because the Airforce waiting list was so long. Then she decided on the Army. I was so against it. Not because I did not believe she could succeed at it but because I wouldn't say I liked the stigma that came with black women in the Army. For starters, they could not achieve high rank without opening their legs, and some saw them as less valuable on the battlefield and weak that they may not value assets because they did not know much. Was any of this true? There is a long list of successful black women in the military of all branches to prove this harsh stereotype wrong, beginning with my mother. I did not want others to use and abuse her in a sense, treat her differently, and be held under toxic leadership or feel like being my wife, she shouldn't have to get her hands dirty, stay out in the field during training exercises, or have to deploy. All these things that I felt like women should not have to do who can also come across alpha males in the military who believe their shit doesn't stink and they say the wrong thing to her now, I'm involved, and from there, it gets ugly for that person cause it sure wouldn't be me that it got ugly for. I felt like I worked hard so she should not have to do these things, and the truth is I was just overly protective when it came down to her. Ultimately, she insisted that this was something she wanted to do and accomplish. From there, I had no choice but to support her as she did me. Isn't that something?

I had known about the military spouse since September 2020, when I was leaving for Afghanistan for a government contract. Shortly after, in October, she would be going for basic training, where she joined as a 35F Intelligence Analysis and where her whole dorm caught Covid. Still, thankfully they were all okay, and why does it seem like I'm always leaving for overseas in September right before her birthday? At times I even felt like the Army pulled me away so much for deployments that it put a strain on my relationship. I mean, out of the six-half years I served, half of that was spent overseas back and forth, and I mean, that must be tough on a person, right? I never said throughout these seven years we were perfect, and quite frankly, if you're able to show me a perfect relationship, I could show you a bold face lie at the same time. I mean, our life literally evolved around one another since we were nineteen years old; wow, that sounds crazy to say now in the year 2022, you know, when you get to reminiscing and thinking, man, we've come a long way that's what I just did. Of course, this journey came with tears, but this time, at a rocky point in our marriage, we had one year it made me cry. This was when I had never seen her respond like this, her words got less, and she was standing on everything she was saying and leaving. She was done for good. I mean, what was I supposed to do? This was the only person I knew; I mean, she was there every step of the way for the man I had grown to become today. No one dealt with the behind-the-scenes of some of my lowest weakest points in life giving up but her, my aid just like Queen Isabella to her husband King Ferdinand, who had inspired the queen chess piece in the game of chest. This patch was not sitting right with me, and yes, I shed tears behind it while listening to R Kelly when a women's fed up.

Fun fact; I'm a true sucker for love. Through it all thus far, we've always seemed to rise to the occasion and fight for what means the most to us while learning something significant that I never understood. You must make yourself happy first before you can begin to enjoy happiness with someone else; otherwise, it just is not fair. I remember our trip out to New Orleans, where we stayed at the Royal Sonesta, another place that's highly recommended for traveling to and a place to stay. The restaurants and food spots we visited were beyond amazing and deserved revisiting. I must admit I wasn't the traveling man. She helped changed my view on that and her mother to get out and make memories and enjoy the beautiful places life has to offer and that it was too precious not to.

Even though I'm late to the party, traveling began for me, and I love it. Our most recent trip to New Orleans in March of 2022, March 17th, Saint Patrick's Day weekend on my dad's birthday, made her happy. Her facial expressions said it all, and that's the look I was going for, all while riding electric scooters through the city and to Saks Fifth Avenue, where we ended up leaving with more clothes and shoes than we came with. Throughout the years, our hard work was beginning to pay off, and shopping more and more was becoming our thing, especially out in Nashville, TN was not too far from there in Tennessee right outside of Fort Campbell, where she got stationed, which lay on the border of Kentucky and Tennessee. I remember going to Nashville and staying at the JW Marriott penthouse to enjoy a few days in the city, and I was on her wrong side, so we just needed the breath of fresh air anyway. During this time, Gucci was one of our favorite stores, and we would spend thousands in that place a little too much, honestly. Now, my wife loves these high-dollar things, but for some reason, or maybe it's just me, she never seems to get around to wearing them like the Louis Vuitton heels and clothes and everything else in her closet that still has the tag on them we should take back to the store right? What If she took the last size of something that someone else wanted and needed to wear for dinner or something, and it's just been sitting in her closet for months and even over a year? I mean, call them collectibles along with the purses at this point, or maybe because it's not that she's in the Army and where a uniform Monday through Friday now.

This explains the Apple of my Eye in a nutshell unless this chapter would never be ending, but to someone who may read this one day, I'm sure it's not hard to tell just by reading about someone you've never met the courageous, loving, caring person she is with a heart full of gold. Besides that, once, she made me cry while threatening to leave and for anyone to stay off her wrong side. No lie, you may think my ambition is unmatched. You should see hers. She is super competitive, and I've seen her upset for not getting an A on a test before instead of a B, and from there, she treated the class like she had a point to prove. Failure is not an option for her, and that's where we match the energy; well, maybe not so much because I would've been okay with a B or even a C grade if we were being honest as long as I passed the class. I remember going to the Opryland Water Park out in Nashville and her trying to race me down the water slides or sitting poolside.

She wanted to play me over and over in a corn hole until she finally beat me, which she did, and I was not handing any wins over easy or letting her win at anything just because we were married. No, ma'am, you want it to earn it. That's how it had always been. She knew she could have anything in the world if I had anything to do with it, but it didn't mean she wasn't going to be something of herself achieving her own goals and working for things she wanted in life, so I guess having me was just a plus. You know how good it feels not to always have to be the one spending money or at dinner in these expensive restaurants because food has gotten expensive? I mean, a cold glass of water isn't even free anymore but to have someone say, no, you don't, not this time. I got the tab.

To the Apple of my eye, hopefully, this letter finds you well, so here goes nothing; you're the most extraordinary woman I have ever met. I'm utterly grateful for you while you've made my life easier. Your selfless efforts make me love you more. Think back on the woman you've grown to become and how much you've accomplished in life, with still so much more in store to offer. I always used to laugh and say, you're like the greatest thing that ever happened to me, but it's no joke; I find that to be true for many reasons. To love and know you, I can't help but be proud and your number one fan with my support with anything you set out to conquer in life. Could we call this a fairytale and happily ever after, true love? No, I'm not sure, but I'm convinced that what we have is something special, and so far, the old saying we used to say back in 2015, "Forever and a day," is still valid. To someone who may read this one day, it's no secret that she's always been the most real one on my team.

"So it's not going to be easy. It's going to be hard. We'll have to work on this daily, but I want to do that because I want you. I want all of you, FOREVER."

- The Notebook

CHAPTER

10

GIA

I was sitting at my in-laws' dinner table in a conversation with my mother-in-law, sister-in-law, and wife. Somehow, I had wind up in a conversation I would rather not be in. We were talking about relationships, and the question arose about putting my homeboys over my actual wife. In my defense, I was debating with my mother-in-law and sister-in-law about my reason for the sacrifices I would make for my homeboys and the things I would do for them if they called on me, even if it put my life in jeopardy or caused me prison time. First thing first, who did I think I was during this time? This was the concept and code I lived by. I was not turning my back on my homies in the hood; if they needed me, I would be the front line no matter the consequences because I was close with my homies, and I knew they would be there for me. Now let's call an apple an apple. This was simply immature thinking but not anything I'm ashamed of or regret; why? Because it's what helped mold me into becoming the man I am today.

Could you imagine how boring life would be if I was perfect? Like if I did everything right, there would be no need to show gratitude or thank God for growth right. My wife never said a word, and who knows what she was thinking then? She always knew how I felt about different things, so maybe she was accepting me as I am, with the understanding he'll get there. He has some maturing to do mentally. Either way, it goes. I was talking crazy and out of my mind. It was complete nonsense. I mean, you would risk it all behind your friends and ruin everything. Those aren't your friends because they should never put you in a situation to do such things. What's unfortunate is a huge percentage of men around the world think this same way, too many to count and too many to name. Unintentionally, we would neglect loved ones for our friends, I don't believe it's intentional at all, but just something that I believe most men feel is a natural thing to do to stay in the good graces of your friends or show that you're still down even after trying to evolve in life. My mother-in-law tried her best to get me to understand that day, but I just couldn't. I wasn't ready, my brain was still locked in that box, and the lack of mental expansion does us more harm than good. This was only the first of many deep intellectual conversations we would have, and let's say it was not easy getting here. I was so much of an introvert in the beginning I did not even care to be around my in-laws. Nope, I don't want to attend family functions or watch NFL Sunday overcome beer with your dad. Mane was I a pain in the ass, these people loved me, and my thought process was now, I'm good. I instead go racing or something to the track with the fellas. Not once was I judged but always embraced, and besides, my mother-in-law was always talking about happiness and peace tapping into your inner self. I always thought my mother-in-law and father-in-law lived a fairy tale life, like what are these people talking about and why they were always so happy. They love traveling and have already been to numerous other countries. They were, in fact living the good life still to this day. My stubborn spider senses always kicked in. What's so special about traveling, I would think, I will instead be in the south. That's what made me, and that's who I was. It was no such thing as true happiness and being at peace within yourself first; what does she mean about all this positive energy law of attraction talk? It was very contradictory for me not to believe in any of that, in the beginning, to say I was married, huh?

Here we go thanking God for growth again. Eventually, she became my outlet and go-to for specific life advice I knew she excelled in. That's right. Even when her daughter was working my last nerve, I would pick up the phone and tell her about it. Honestly, she became like the family therapist; everyone was always bringing their problems and venting to her. The heart she has and the love she gives for those around her are unmatched, but I'm sure some days she got tired of us all without saying it, as I'm sure my father-in-law O.G was her shoulder to lean on in her demanding days. I, in my mind, would question everything she did for her two daughters and grandson Jojo. I mean, she was like the woman superman superwoman, the definition of giving the shirt off her back for her loved ones.

Living in North Carolina, I guarantee you if her grandson called crying, missing his gandma (yup, that's what he calls her gandma), she's calling out of work and jumping on the road that same day to her daughter's house in Suffolk Virginia to wipe the tears from his eyes. Now, if that's not incredible, get a load of this; my wife needed her one day for something that required my mother-in-law. Could it have waited? Well, it could have, but what did my mother-in-law do? Book a flight and come to town, like, what's up? I'm here to rescue. The things she does for the ones she loves; I can go on and on. The stories are phenomenal and mind-blowing. The same rules applied to best believe if I'm calling, she's answering or getting back to me shortly. I remember she would always say she loved me and I was her son-in-law forever, no matter what happened between her daughter and me. Yup, guys, news flash if things were ever to go left, I'd still be a part of the family forever, so don't even thank about it; I'm still at all the thanksgiving dinners and handing out gifts to my nephew at Christmas, who's now has developed an obsession for sneakers and becoming a sneakerhead. I knew my in-laws loved me when recently, in the year 2022, while my wife was deployed to Poland, I suffered a weak point and the tears began to fall from missing my father, and unfortunately, Heaven did not have a phone line I could call. What did I do? Speed dialed my father-in-law in the hours of the morning, around midnight. Knowing he had work in the morning, he answered the phone, allowed me to vent, and reminded me that he had me and everything was going to be alright. The words coming from him, "I got you," touched my soul, and I instantly started to feel better; it's just a different type of feeling when someone genuinely cares about your well-being and stands in your corner that's all, especially coming from a man of few words. That is, until he's enjoying himself with his family over a few drinks. Then, this man becomes hilarious, I'm talking about a full-blown comedian, and he is a joy to be around cooking on that high-dollar grille. He's my cryptocurrency and financial advisor, aka the nerd of the family, financials, and credit advice; he has the answers and a credit score so high that I did not even know credit scores could go that high. My in-laws were all great in their way and knew how to have a good time. I remember my mother-in-law's nephew came to town; during this time, my father-in-law was doing a year tour in Korea. One night while up playing trouble board game with my wife, mother-in-law, her nephew, and sister-in-law and playing old school jams while the stove smells lovely with good eats. Man, we were in our little world that night, I mean, getting drunk as ever; I mean, you just had to be there every three minutes. Someone would yell shot-ah-clock! And it was time to take another shot! Back-to-back, like the drake song, her nephew and I were on Hennessey, my favorite at the time, while they were on Patron, my wife's favorite, a man by the end of the night, my mother-in-in-law was so drunk she just made her way to her main bedroom. Well, at least we thought she was sleeping until her daughters checked on her, and she was taking a cat nap on her bathroom floor; this was too funny, and she had out herself. So, of course, they got her in bed, and that was that as the next day she woke up back to her normal self as if nothing had happened, but that was a great memory, and that night we all enjoyed ourselves, and I kicked butt in trouble boardgame. Okay, maybe I'm fabricating things a little there, but this is my story. I can tell it how I please. Throughout all the great memories we all share, it was my mother-in-law that helped with my mental expansion. She would say like this "Attract what you expect, reflect what you desire, become what you respect, mirror what you admire." The younger me would say this made no sense; however, today, it means perfect sense. She always challenged me to read books like the law of attraction and the seven spiritual laws of success. I highly recommend those books are life-changing and show you that the energy you put out is what you receive. Life is what you make it; be like my in-laws, travel, and be glad in the life the man above gave you and rejoice in it. I was no longer the little boy locked mentally in that brown box, I had broadened my horizon, and my thought process on life began to develop differently. Just like my mother-in-law tried to assure me in the beginning, there was such a thing as inner peace and happiness within yourself that was no one else's job, but yours, the transformation of energy was, in fact, a real thing. It felt good and honestly just like a breath of fresh air when walking outside on a beautiful day where the weather is just right, not too cold or hot, but when the weather is just right. Mentally life was changing for me, and it's a special reward. My mother-in-law would earn the deserving nickname Gia from me, a girl's name of Italian Origin, meaning "God is Gracious." A derivative of Giovanna means "God's gracious gift." This was how much my mother-in-law meant to me. She was my go-to, my Gia, God's gracious gift to me, so if you ever get to meet her one day, know that she's now known as Gia.

"I love you, not because you are my mother-in-law; but because you are God's Gracious Gift to me"

— Markus Cuttino.

CHAPTER 11

NOTE TO SELF

Did you know that more than half of the men globally are less likely to engage in help-seeking behavior and downplay their physical and mental health symptoms because of stereotypes like it'll make you look weak? Unaddressed relational problems, addictions, and traumas include depression, anxiety, and sleep insomnia worsening over time. Men associate seeking assistance for psychological or emotional problems with shame or weakness, which is unfortunate but true. Realistic speaking is portrayed as trying to be muscular, tough, macho, and manly, avoiding problems, ignoring pain, and denying reality. In return, well, what does this affect? I thought you'd never ask in return; this correlates with serious health issues, especially in the cardiovascular department and immune system. This way of thinking and self-destructive behavior leads to unhealthy lifestyles and chronic stress that, over time, could very much so be detrimental.

In Mr. Jason Wilson's book Emotional Incarceration, he compares this mental state to a typical prison cell which is about 6-8ft, cased in steel walls and barred with a cell door. Mr. Wilson tells us about emotional incarceration now; this prison cell is quite different. It holds more men captive than all actual physical industrial prisons built worldwide. Unlike the physical prison, this incarceration locks from the inside by voluntarily victims being Men who choose to turn themselves in mentally. Mr. Jason Wilson describes emotional incarceration as a self-imposed mental prison that confines a man to nine masculine emotions and isolates his heart from the world. Due to the lack of safe spaces to express our emotions, we stay incarcerated to avoid being humiliated for just trying to be human. As he referred to one of Drakes's lyrics, "I pop bottles because I bottle my emotions," but what we don't realize by, in fact, doing this when life gets to the point of being simply too much we can bear, we pop and explode just like a shaken-up bottle. In countries worldwide, suicide for men is three times as much for women. Why? Well, it's no simple answer there, but it certainly has a lot to do with men not wanting to feel vulnerable. Biochemist Dr. William H. Frey discovered that emotionally induced tears contain not only water but stress hormones that are released from the body through crying. Just like Mr. Wilson reminded us who read his book and watched him speak, take a moment to write these questions down and answer them to yourself and even go the extra mile by sharing if you're up to it that he recommended. What emotions keep you emotionally imprisoned daily? What are the events in your life that led you to incarcerate yourself emotionally? And lastly, what areas in your life do you need to achieve victory, and what do you need to do to start waging and winning the inner war to attain it? Wow, and hats off to Mr. Jason Wilson, we need more of this, and it just had to be said. Permanent scars encapsulate a young boy to an adult who was still emotionally incarcerated and had no identity coming from the streets of South Carolina. We were raised to think men are tough. We don't cry. Crying makes you weak. It's no reason why I lost my dad at the age of twelve, and at that very moment felt like I had to be strong and a man at the age of twelve to protect and stand up for those around me. Also, who created this stereotype anyway for little boys don't cry, men don't have emotions, simply annihilating boys to men humanity and sending them on a long ride of years of emotional incarceration that some don't always return from.

Without a doubt, I can confidently say that every man today in my hood would benefit from mental therapy. I mean were surrounded by nothing by poverty, low-income or dead-end jobs, and death, and that's to name a few, so how could they not, right? It's survival of the fittest out there, you know. Get it how you live the type of thing, and not everyone will be as fortunate as me and others who made it out. I carried being emotionally incarcerated until the age of twenty-seven because, for one, I did not know any better, which is extremely not okay because I was always telling everyone knowledge is power. Still, as the good saying goes, it's better late than never. So, it's only right that I give to someone who may read this one day another story inside of a story, right? Well, remember September 2020 to May 2021, one of the worse nine months of my life when I was contracting in Afghanistan, and it damn near broke me. Well, thank God I was a veteran and could call the Veteran hotline and be appointed a therapist. I did not know much of what to say, but I knew I needed help. I could not take it anymore; it was just too many things bottled up inside, and just like Mr. Jason Wilson said, eventually, you would be ready to pop, just like that same bottle Drake was referring to in his song. This was me, but it was an older lady named Dr. McCune. She spoke so softly and sentimentally in her voice. However, I still was afraid that she would not understand where I was coming from because her life did not relate to mine, or we had not been through the same things in life. Little did I know, I did not need someone who went through exactly what I had been through but, most importantly, a listening ear, and this was not, in fact, her first rodeo. She knew what was considered to be permanent scars and what that felt like for people. She was an impeccable listener, and the way she articulated things was even better. So many wows, and that's amazing. I did not even think about it like that. Late August, Early September 2022, to my surprise, I still had her number, and I took it upon myself to reach out and thank her, showing excessive gratitude. Again, to my surprise, being an impeccable listener was not the only thing she was good at but also an amazing memory. This lady remembered every telephonic therapy session we had as if the conversation had touched her. Right then and there, I knew firsthand that this was more than a job for her, and having her as a therapist was to my luck. She reminded me of breathing exercises and was amazed at the dark hole I had climbed out of and told me she knew I could do it all along. She was only there as a listening ear and supplying the tools I needed to help in my journey. Those with the courage to admit they need help and self-healing mentally is the first tough step, so to recognize that on your own, I knew you would be just fine. This made my day even more, when she detailed my thinking and the dark words I would use to describe my emotional incarceration back then to what I was slowly becoming today, emotional freedom with self-identity. Summer 2022 was also the year I discovered Dr. Joe Dispenza. This man was speaking all around the world on the mental functions of the membrane. Where was I? stuck under a rock or something. I mean, was I the only one who had not heard of the great books he had written, Becoming Supernatural, Breaking the Habit of Being Yourself, Evolve your Brain, also mediation guides such as Generating Abundance, Morning and Evening and You Are the Placeboes to name a few. How you think and feel creates a human state of being. Okay, now, Dr. Dispenza, what do you mean by that? Well, in a nutshell, what he meant by this, and I challenge someone who may read this one day to look deeper into this, but what he is referring to is this. Separating the unconscious mind, which is your body, versus the subconscious mind, which is your brain. Did you know that over the years, our body develops bad habits that, over time, we become used to and naturally begin to think it's right and see no problem with it? This is the unconscious mind taking over. It does not need your subconscious mind or brain to tell it what to do anymore. Those bad habits are already developed for so long that your body already knows what you're going to do even before you do it. Think of it as your first day in the gym. For those not used to working out, your first day in the gym after a good workout, you would most likely become very sore. It's something different that your body is not used to. Meditation helps separate the two consciousness by controlling what you can control. Dr. Joe Dispenza does a great job of helping us to understand what's important, and that's that your emotions control your thoughts, your thoughts control your behaviors, and lastly, your behaviors control your actions. What can you control, you ask? Well, your boundaries, thoughts and actions, goals you set, what you give your energy to, how you speak to yourself, and how you handle challenges. Now, you cannot control those people often sometimes, including me. Yes, I'm guilty at times and still learning. Still, hey, to someone who may read this one day, you cannot control the past, what happens around you, what other people may think of you, the outcome of efforts, how others choose to take care of themselves, the opinions of others and not even the action of others. Therapy is a journey that many humans often shy away from for various personal reasons, but it can be very beneficial. This note to self was very much so personal and a reminder of how far I've come mentally, not ever to relapse, and how I cope with the permanent scars I've personally encountered in life. I can do it by any means necessary. Today, I even have a short thirty-minute therapy session once a month telephonic to have a known outlet of being able to express myself when needed, and an emotional incarceration is no longer an option for me. Just like we said no to drugs, I had escaped emotional incarceration, and this was my note to self.

"Shallow men believe in luck and circumstances; strong men believe in cause and effect. The best way to predict your future is to create it, so you should leave nothing to chance."

— Ralph Waldo Emerson.

CHAPTER

12

WHAT IT MEANS TO BE KING

Finally, to someone who may read this one day, if you're here well, you've read the journey thus far of Markus Cuttino and my autobiography Permanent Scars. I start my day between 4:30 AM and 5:00 AM central time every morning with no alarm clock. My ambition and hunger to keep going and evolving awaken me. Why do I start my day this early? Well, that answer is quite simple, and it's because it's more peaceful at this time. The rest of the world is still sleeping. So I go right into a meditation on my bedroom floor in a cross-legged Indian-style position. I know now it's time just to let my brain wander off somewhere far-far away to outer space. For these moments, nothing else matters; deep breaths in, deep breaths out, and silence and meditation. I love it; I can hear a pin drop on the carpet in this place. I jump to my feet and instantly begin to show gratitude to the man above for allowing me to see another day with another shot at being better than I was yesterday. By now, I'm in my bathroom mirror brushing my teeth and doing my daily morning facial cleansing routine while listening to my favorite motivational speaker Eric Thomas aka the Hip Hop Preacher, aka He's motivation. This is bound to get me excited for the start of a great productive day; my Gia always told me not to let anyone steal my thunder.

After a banging workout in the gym, I'm back home, showering and having breakfast before I sit in my office chair at my desk to log in for work. I usually eat a big bowl of cereal, French Toast Crunch to be exact, hmmm hmmm good, yum, my favorite. Today, I'm in a career field I never saw coming, you know, doing Software Engineer things in technology, the security operations department handling all cybersecurity incidents and tasks. That accomplishment goes in the top tier bag of one of my proudest achievements and thankful moments. I think I was slowly figuring this thing called life out; that's right first thing first, perseverance, which is the persistence in doing something despite difficulty or delay in achieving success. See, there was, in fact, no me without perseverance. I gave you numerous permanent scars that I could've given up long ago. As a child, I was on an asthma machine every night before bed and spent some nights in the hospital. At ages eleven, twelve, and thirteen, I constantly lost father figures who meant the world to me. Perseverance got me through; it was too easy to fall in line with the other statistics that would fit my profile of a little brown boy from the hood that amounted to nothing.

It's easy to amount to nothing and sit on your ass all day, every day, but what's hard is the person who wants it, the single parent that gets up every day and makes it happen for their child, the adults who held a job all their life waking up going to work and most often a place they wish not to be. However, bills are still due on the first. What about the college student who's about to take the biggest exam of their life, whose future and dream career depend on it? What about the people who have the determination and keep going time and time again when they feel like they cannot catch a break, like the new entrepreneur who's trying to establish a profitable business for everyone around the globe who just was not as fortunate as others and have what may seem like every possible reason to quit, perseverance that is I tell you, such a beautiful thing. Secondly, Gratitude is the quality of being thankful and ready to show appreciation for and to return kindness. See, I felt like I worked for it, so what was the point of being grateful or deserving? I mean, I did deserve it. I worked for it, right? Not that I did work hard for the man I was becoming; however, how can you continue growing and enjoying the fruits of labor life does have to offer if you're not even thankful for what you do have? Trust me, I've tried, and it does not work, and the saying it could always be a lot worse, or someone is going through worse, is very true. So, gratitude, be thankful for the season you're in and allow yourself to trust the process. Unfortunately, no matter how we feel, it does not happen overnight. Remember, we must control what we can control, and according to the law of attraction, the energy you give will be exactly the energy you receive in return.

Permanent Scars from trauma and things I faced throughout my life were causing me to self-destruct, and it wasn't that I needed to forget what I had been through but learn how to cope with these permanent scars and move forward. Release whatever anger, trauma, or anything damaging may be bottled up inside your heart to move forward with your seasons in life. You know, the peace, love, and happiness movement type of thing, understanding that change is uncomfortable but necessary and the other end feels astonishing, you know, just like the light at the end of the tunnel methodology. You've got to know and maybe even read this line twice if you have to, but "nothing changes if nothing changes" is short, simple, and sweet, right? How do you expect better or anything to change when you're not ready to commit and sacrifice what it takes to reach the next level in all aspects of life? A wise man once told me one day that this may even require losing family and friends, and if they did not understand where you were going in life, then they probably weren't meant for you anyway. Everyone you started with, you won't see the finish line with, and that's just as about as straightforward as it gets. Sometimes you must stop the elevator and let certain people of that mean you are no good or cannot see the vision as you close the doors and allow the elevator to continue taking you up. It's called trusting the process. You guys are now in different rooms and are no longer beneficial to each other. You know, in reality, doing more harm than good. Now I can happily take my advice because before, I struggled with letting certain friends, family, and people go, but it's the nature of the beast. Whoever told you that you could have your cake and eat it too, they lied. It's not true. We want to take everyone on our evolving journey. Never block your blessings by trying to force good intentions on others and let alone get them to see what you see. You know that thing about positive energy we discussed, the seven spiritual laws of success? It must be natural, I tell you, natural! Thank you to someone who may read this one day. Hopefully, you enjoyed it, and I'm forever grateful for the support. To my father and others, I've lost to the graveyard, it still hurts like hell, and some days I still cry behind it, but in the end, I'm okay and still pushing on. To anyone that looked up to me as their role model and reached out to let me know the light they saw me in, well, the truth is people like you all are, in fact, my motivation and something I'm genuinely thankful for wholeheartedly. To anyone in the world who may be waiting or silently praying about my downfall, I wouldn't hold my breath on that one too long. This was God's Plan, and only a select few are among the chosen ones. Thank God, my mother and father, for laying down and making me. Now, I can say I took so many losses and can't believe I finally got to win. This is all of what it means to be King.

"People look at you strange saying you changed like we work this hard to remain the same"

- Shawn Corey Carter (Jay-z)